THE GREAT COMMISSION

A SERMON

COLLECTION

Charles H. Spurgeon

THE GREAT
COMMISSION

Introduction by JASON K. ALLEN

PUBLISHING
BRENTWOOD, TENNESSEE

978-1-0877-8451-9

Published by B&H Publishing Group
Brentwood, Tennessee

Dewey Decimal Classification: 269.2
Subject Heading: SPURGEON, CHARLES
HADDON / GREAT COMMISSION (BIBLE)—
SERMONS / EVANGELISTIC WORK

All Scripture references are taken from the
King James Version; public domain.

Cover design by B&H Publishing Group.
Cover image by Photo 12 / Alamy Stock Photo.

All Spurgeon sermons used are public domain.

1 2 3 4 5 6 • 28 27 26 25 24

CONTENTS

Introduction

Jason K. Allen

Since he burst onto the scene in mid-nineteenth-century London, Charles Spurgeon's name has been synonymous with faithful, convictional gospel ministry. And though Spurgeon's power in the pulpit remains the hallmark of his ministry, the great preacher's commitment to the Great Commission is ever-inspiring as well.

Throughout his pastorate at the Metropolitan Tabernacle, Spurgeon consistently thundered forth the gospel message. Beyond the pulpit, Spurgeon launched some sixty-six additional ministries throughout his life. Each of these ministries had an ultimate end in mind—introducing people to Spurgeon's Saviour, Jesus Christ.

More broadly, Spurgeon's ministry was a global ministry because his message was a global message. Spurgeon believed in the exclusivity of the gospel of Jesus Christ, proclaiming that every person must repent of their sins and consciously place their faith in Christ for salvation. Thus, Spurgeon's gospel gaze rose beyond his London parishioners to across the seas and unto distant lands. Spurgeon intended his ministry for all peoples of the Earth because the gospel is meant for all the peoples of the Earth.

Indeed, Spurgeon was a natural evangelist, one who saw a harvest of souls under his ministry in London, and from his ministry the world over. Weekly, Spurgeon's sermons were transcribed, edited, and disseminated through the tentacles of the British Empire—which then spanned the globe. Wherever you found a Spurgeon sermon you found a gospel message.

A Welsh minister remarked that as every English town and village had a road to London, "so from every text in Scripture there is a road to the metropolis of the Scriptures, that is Christ. . . . I have never yet found a text that had not got a road to Christ in it, but if I ever do find one that has not got a road to Christ in it, I will make one." And Spurgeon did just that. From every text and in every sermon, he, indeed, made "a road to Christ."[1]

But don't take my word for it. Pull off the shelf any one of the sixty-three volumes of Spurgeon's *Metropolitan Tabernacle Pulpit* and flip to any sermon printed within it. Then, turn to the end of that sermon. If Spurgeon doesn't end with a word about Christ, it's because he already pointed his listeners to his Lord in the preceding paragraphs.

Though Spurgeon was singular in his gifting, his commitment to the Great Commission should resonate with every Christian. Every believer stands as a member of Christ's intended audience when he charged his disciples to, "Go therefore and make disciples of all the nations, baptizing them in the name of the Father and the Son and the Holy Spirit, teaching them to observe all that I commanded you; and lo, I am with you always, even to the end of the age" (Matt. 28:19–20).

When believers look for their purpose in life, they should look to the Great Commission. When ministers look for what should animate their ministry, they should look to the Great Commission. And

---

1. Charles Spurgeon, "Christ Precious to Believers," *Metropolitan Tabernacle Pulpit*, Vol. 5, Sermon 242, 237.

when churches look for a mission statement, they should look to the Great Commission. The Great Commission is to be our mission.

In this sense, we all are to be Spurgeonesque, devoted to spreading the gospel of Christ. To this end, we can find no better role model than Charles Haddon Spurgeon. And that's why I compiled the sermons in this book. It comes to you with a prayer that God will use this small volume to instigate a great work—the broader proclamation of the gospel, and a greater urgency to fulfill the Great Commission.

And, I trust, that as you read these curated sermons from Spurgeon, you'll not only sense his Great Commission fervor, but you'll also rekindle your own. That's what we need. That's what you need. Enjoy, this book, dear reader, and may you make more of Jesus as you do.

The Missionaries' Charge and Charts[2]

*"And Jesus came and spake unto them, saying,
'All power is given unto me in heaven and in
earth. Go ye therefore, and teach all nations,
baptizing them in the name of the Father,
and of the Son, and of the Holy Spirit.'"*
(Matthew 28:18–19)

While I was meditating in private upon this
text, I felt myself carried away by its power.
I was quite unable calmly to consider its terms or to

---

2. Published in *Metropolitan Tabernacle Pulpit*, Vol. 7 in 1861 by Charles Spurgeon. This is sermon 383, delivered on April 21, 1861.

investigate its argument. The command with which the text concludes repeated itself again and again and again in my ears, till I found it impossible to study, for my thoughts were running here and there, asking a thousand questions, all of them intended to help me in answering for myself the solemn enquiry, "How am I to go and teach all nations, baptizing them in the name of the Father, and of the Son, and of the Holy Spirit?"

The practical lesson seemed to me to overwhelm in my mind the argument of which that lesson is but a conclusion, "Go and teach all nations." My ears seemed to hear it as if Christ were then speaking it to me. I could realize his presence by my side. I thought I could see him lift his pierced hand and hear him speak, as he was wont to speak, with authority blended with meekness, "Go and teach all nations, baptizing them in the name of the all-glorious God." Oh! I would that the church could hear the Savior addressing these words to her now, for the words of Christ are living words, not having power in them yesterday alone, but today also. The injunctions of the Savior are perpetual in their obligation; they were not binding upon apostles merely but upon us also and upon every Christian does this yoke fall, "Go, therefore, and teach all nations, baptizing them in the name of the Father, and of the Son, and of the Holy Spirit." We are not exempt today from the service of the first followers of the Lamb. Our marching orders are the same as theirs, and our Captain requires from us obedience as prompt and perfect as from them. Oh that his message may not fall upon deaf ears or be heard by stolid souls!

Brothers, the heathen are perishing; shall we let them perish? His name is blasphemed; shall we be quiet and still? The honor of Christ is cast into the dust and his foes revile his person and resist his throne; shall we his soldiers suffer this and not find our hands feeling for the hilt of our sword, the sword of the Spirit, which is the Word of God? Our Lord delays his coming; shall we begin to sleep, or to eat, or to be drunken? Shall we not rather gird up the loins of our mind and cry unto him, "Come, Lord Jesus, come quickly"?

The scoffing skeptics of these last days have said that the anticipated conquest of the world for Christ is but a dream, or an ambitious thought, which crossed our leader's mind but which never is to be accomplished. Some assert that the superstitions of the heathen are too strong to be battered down by our teachings and that the strongholds of Satan are utterly impregnable against our attacks. Shall it be so?

Shall we be content foolishly to sit still? Nay, rather let us work out the problem; let us prove the promise of God to be true; let us prove the words of Jesus to be words of soberness; let us show the efficacy of his blood and the invincibility of his Spirit by going in the spirit of faith, teaching all nations, and winning them to the obedience of Christ our Lord.

I do not know how to begin to preach this morning, but still it seems to me, standing here, as if I heard that voice saying, "Go, therefore, and teach all nations." And my soul sometimes pants and longs for the liberty to preach Christ where he was never preached before, not to build upon another man s foundation but to go to some untrodden land, some waste where the foot of Christ's minister was never seen, that there "the meditary place might be glad for us, and the wilderness rejoice and blossom as the rose."

I have made it a solemn question whether I might not testify in China or India the grace of Jesus, and in the sight of God I have answered it. I solemnly feel that my position in England will not permit my leaving the sphere in which I now am, or else tomorrow I would offer myself as a missionary. Oh, do none of you hear the call this morning? You who are free from so great a work as that which is cast upon me, you who have talents as yet undevoted to any special end and powers of being as yet unconsecrated to any given purpose and unconfined to any one sphere, do you not hear my Master saying, in tones of plaintive sorrow blended with an authority which is not to be denied, " Go, therefore, and teach all nations, baptizing them in the name of the Father, and of the Son, and of the Holy Spirit"?

Oh that I could preach like Peter the Hermit—a better crusade than he! Oh that there were might in some human lip to move the thousands of our Israel to advance at once, unanimously and irresistibly to the world's conquest, like one tremendous tide rising from the depths of the ocean to sweep over the sands, the barren sands that are now given up to desolation and death! Oh that once again the voice of thunder could be heard and the lightning spirit could penetrate each heart, that as one man the entire Church might take the marching orders of her Lord and go teach all nations, baptizing them in the name of Israel's God! O Lord, if we fail to speak, fail not you to speak, and if we know not how to bear your burden or express your awful thoughts, yet speak with that all-constraining silent voice that well-trained ears can hear, and make your servants obedient to you now, for Christ's sake!

Awake, thou Spirit, who of old
Didst fire the watchman of the Church's
 youth,
Who faced the foe, unshrinking, bold,
Who witness'd day and night the eternal
 truth,
Whose voices through the world are ring-
 ing still,
And bringing hosts to know and do your
 will!

Oh that your fire were kindled soon,
That swift from land to land its flame
 might leap!
Lord, give us but this priceless boon
Of faithful servants, fit for you to reap
The harvest of the soul; look down and view
How great the harvest, yet the laborers
 few.

Oh haste to help ere we are lost!
Send forth evangelists, in spirit strong,
Arm'd with your Word, a dauntless host,
Bold to attack the rule of ancient wrong;
And let them all the earth for you reclaim,
To be your kingdom, and to know your
 name.

This morning we shall first dwell a little while upon the command, and then, secondly, we shall enlarge upon the argument. There is an argument, as you will perceive, "Go, therefore, and teach all nations."

The Command

First, my brothers, and very briefly indeed, a few things about the command. And we must remark, first, what a singularly loving one it is. Imagine Muhammad on his dying bed saying to his disciples, "All power is given unto me in heaven and in earth." What would be his command? "Go, therefore, with sharp scimitars, and propound faith in the prophet, or death as the dread alternative; avenge me of the men who threw stones at the prophet; make their houses a dunghill and cut them in pieces, for vengeance is mine, and God's prophet must be avenged of his enemies."

But Christ, though far more despised and persecuted of men, and having a real power that that pretended prophet never had, says to his disciples as he is about to ascend to heaven, "All power is given unto me in heaven and in earth; go, therefore, and teach all nations, baptizing them in the name of the Father, and of the Son, and of the Holy Spirit." It is the voice of love, not of wrath. "Go and teach them the power of my blood to cleanse, the willingness of my arms to embrace, the yearning of my heart to save! Go and teach them. Teach them no more to despise me, no more to think my Father an angry and implacable Deity. Teach them to 'bow the knee, and kiss the Son' and find peace for all their troubles and a balm for all their woes in me. Go; speak as I have spoken; weep as I have wept; invite as I have invited; exhort, entreat, beseech and pray as I have done before you. Tell them to come unto me, if they are weary and heavy laden, and I will give them rest. And say unto them, 'I have no pleasure in the death of him that dies but had rather that he should turn unto me and live.'" What a generous and gracious command is that of the text, "Go, therefore, and teach all nations, baptizing them in the name of the Father, and of the Son, and of the Holy Spirit."

Note, too, how exceedingly plain is the command, "Go, teach all nations." The Romish Church has misunderstood this. She says, "Go, mystify all nations. Sound in their ears a language once living but now dead. Take to them the Latin tongue, and let that be sounded with all the harmony of sweet music, and they will be converted. Erect the sumptuous altar. Clothe the priest in mystic garments. Celebrate mysterious rites and make the heathen wonder. Dazzle them with splendor; amaze them with mystery." "Nay," says Christ, "nay, go and teach."

Why, it is the mother's work with her child; it is the tutor's work with the boy and with the girl—"go and teach." How simple! Illustrate, explain, expound, tell, inform, narrate. Take from them the darkness of ignorance; reveal to them the light of revelation. Teach! Be content to sit down and tell them the very plainest and most common things. It is not your eloquence that shall convert them; it is not your gaudy language or your polished periods that shall sway their intellects. Go and teach them. Teach them! Why, my hearer, I say again, this is a word that has to do with the rudiments of knowledge. We do not preach to children; we teach them. And we are not so much to preach to nations; that word seems too big and great for the uncivilized and childish people. Go and teach them first the very simplicities of the cross of Christ.

And note how he puts it next. Who are to be taught? "Go and teach all nations." The Greek has his philosophers. Teach him; he is but a child. He is a fool, though he think himself to be wise. There be polite nations that have a literature of their own, far larger and more extensive than the literature of the Christian. Teach them nevertheless; they are to be taught, and unless they are willing to take the learner's place and to become as little children, they can in no wise enter into the kingdom of heaven. Do not debate and argue with them. Put not yourself with them upon their level as a combatant concerning certain dogmas. Insist upon it that I have sent you—sent you to teach the most erudite and profoundly learned. And when you shall claim it, I am with you always to back your claim, and men shall be willing to sit at your feet to be taught the name of Jesus.

I do not know whether all our missionaries have caught the idea of Christ—"Go and teach all nations"—but many of them have, and these have been honored with many conversions. The more fully they have been simple teachers, not philosophers of Western philosophy, not eager disputants concerning some English dogma, I say the more plainly they have gone forth as teachers sent from God to teach the world, the more successful have they been. "Go, therefore, and teach."

Some may think, perhaps, there is less difficulty in teaching the learned than in teaching the uncivilized and barbarous. There is the same duty to the one as to the other: "Go and teach." "But they brandish the tomahawk." Teach them, and lie down and sleep in their hut, and they shall marvel at your fearlessness and spare your life. "But they feed on the blood of their fellows; they make a bloody feast about the cauldron in which a man's body is the horrible viand." Teach them, and they shall empty their war kettle, and they shall bury their swords and bow before you and acknowledge King Jesus. "But they are brutalized; they have scarce a language—a few clicking sounds make up all that they can say." Teach them, and they shall speak the language of Canaan and sing the songs of heaven.

The fact has been proved, brothers, that there are no nations incapable of being taught, nay, that there are no nations incapable afterwards of teaching others. The Negro slave has perished under the lash rather than dishonor his Master. The Innuit has climbed his barren steeps and borne his toil while he has recollected the burden Jesus bore. The Hindu has patiently submitted to the loss of all things because he loved Christ better than all. Feeble Malagasay women have been prepared to suffer and to die and have taken joyfully suffering for Christ's sake.

There has been heroism in every land for Christ. Men of every color and of every race have died for him; upon his altar has been found the blood of all kindreds that are upon the face of the earth. Oh! tell me not they cannot be taught. Sirs, they can be taught to die for Christ, and this is more than some of you have learned. They can rehearse the very highest lesson of the Christian religion—that self-sacrifice that knows not itself but gives up all for him, At this day there are Karen missionaries preaching among the Karens with as fervid an eloquence as ever was known by Whitfield. There are Chinese teaching in Borneo, Sumatra, and Australia with as much earnestness as Morison or Milne first taught in China. There are Hindu evangelists who are not ashamed to have given up the Brahminical thread, and to eat with the Pariah, and to preach with him the riches of Christ. There have been men found of every class and kind, not only able to be taught but able to become teachers themselves, and the most mighty teachers too, of the grace of the Lord Jesus Christ. Well was that command warranted by future facts, when Christ said, "Go, teach all nations."

But, brothers, the text says, "baptizing them" They are to be taught, and afterwards they are to be baptized. I know not why it is that we yield to the superstitions of our Christian brothers so much as to use the word baptize at all. It is not an English but a Greek word. It has but one meaning and cannot bear another. Throughout all the classics, without exception, it is not possible to translate it correctly except with the idea of immersion; and believing this and knowing this, if the translation is not complete, we will complete it this morning. "Go, therefore, and teach all nations, immersing them in the name of the Father, and of the Son, and of the Holy Spirit."

Now, I think that our Missionary Society, while it may take precedence in matters of time—for it was the first that was ever commenced with the exception of the Moravians—ought also to take precedence in matters of purity, because we can carry out this text in every country, teaching first and baptizing afterwards. We do not understand the philosophy of baptizing and afterwards teaching. We hold that we must teach first, and then, when men are discipled, we are to baptize them. Not the nations—the Greek does not bear that interpretation—but those who have been discipled we are to baptize into the sacred Name.

We think that our brothers do serious damage to the gospel by baptizing children. We do not think their error a little one. We know it does not touch a vital point, but we do believe that infant baptism is the prop and pillar of Popery, and it being removed, Popery and Puseyism become at once impossible. You have taken away all idea of a national godliness and a national religion when you have cut away all liberty to administer Christian ordinances to unconverted persons. We cannot see any evil that would follow if our brothers would renounce their mistake, but we can see abundant mischief their mistake has caused, and in all kindness but with all fidelity, we again enter our solemn protest against their giving baptism to any but disciples, to any but those who are the followers of the Lamb.

Throw down her hedges? Give her supper and her baptism to those that are not Christ's people? Break down her walls? Remove her barricades? God forbid! Except a man be renewed in heart, we dare not allow him to participate in the ordinances that belong to Christ's church. Oh! It is a disastrous thing to call unconverted children Christians or to do anything that may weaken their apprehension of the great fact that until they are converted they have no part or lot in this matter.

Brothers, if you differ from me on this point, bear with me, for my conscience will not let me conceal this solemn truth. To you who agree with me I say, while our other friends can do in some things more than we can—and we rejoice in their efforts and would heartily bless God that they have shown more activity than ourselves—yet we ought to be ashamed of ourselves if we are a whit behind. We are a body of Christians who can fairly and purely teach and baptize; we can obey this command of Christ abroad as well as at home without running counter to our practice in one place by our practice in the other. We ought to be first and foremost, and if we are not, shame shall cover us for our unfaithfulness. Again, I say, I hear that voice ringing in the Baptist's ear, above that of any other man, "Go, therefore, and teach all nations, baptizing them in the name of the Father, and of the Son, and of the Holy Spirit."

I have endeavored to be brief, but I find I have been long and therefore pass at once to the argument with which the text commences.

The Argument

The argument is this: "All power is given unto me in heaven and in earth, go, therefore, and teach all nations." Three things here. Christ had suffered, bled and died; he had now risen from the dead. As the effect of his finished work, he had as mediator received all power in heaven and in earth. There is no allusion here to his inherent power that is not given to him; that is his native right. He has, as God, all power in heaven and in earth. The text relates to him as mediator. As mediator he had not this power once; he was weak, he was forsaken even of his God. But now, having finished the work that was given him to do, his Father honors him. He is about to lift him to his right hand and gives him, as the result of resurrection, all power in heaven and in earth. Three things, then. First, this is the picture of the church's history, and therefore she should teach all nations. Secondly, this is the church's right. Thirdly, it is the church's might; and for all these reasons she ought to teach all nations.

First, this is the church's picture. Christ suffers, bleeds, dies. Do you give up his cause? Do you look upon it as forlorn and desolate? He is nailed to the tree; the world abhors him, fools gaze, and sinners laugh. Do you lay down your weapons and say it is idle to defend such a man as this? It is all over now; he bows his head upon the cross. "It is finished," says he, and do your unbelieving hearts say, "Ay, indeed, it is finished; his career is over, his hopes are blighted, his prospects withered"? Ah! Little do you know that his shame was the mother of his future glory, that the stooping was the rising, that the crown of thorns was in fact the fruitful root out of which sprang the eternal crown of glory.

He is put into the grave: do you say that there is the grave of all your faith could believe or your hope could suggest? He rises, brothers, and his resurrection takes effect and fruit from the fact that he died and was buried. Do you not see the picture? We have been sending out heralds of the cross these eighteen hundred years; they have landed upon many a shore to die. Fever has taken off its hundreds; cruel men have slain their score; from the first day until now, the record of the mission is written in blood. Somewhere or other there always must be martyrs for Christ. It seems as if the church never could plough a wave without a spray of gore. She is still in Madagascar persecuted, afflicted, tormented. Still are her ministers hunted about like partridges upon the mountains, and her blood is dying the shambles of her slayers. Do you give up all hope? Shall we, as we look upon the tombs of our missionaries, say that Christ's cause is dead? Brothers, as you turn over the long roll and read the names of one after another who sleep in Jesus, shall you say, "Let us close the doors of the mission house; let us cease our contributions; it is clear the case is hopeless, and the cause can never have success"?

Nay, rather, the church must suffer that she may reign; she must die that she may live; she must be stained with blood that she may be robed in purple; she must go down into the earth, and seem to be buried and forgotten, that the earth may help the woman, that she may be delivered of the man child. Courage! Courage! Courage! The past is hopeful because to the eye it seems hopeless; the cause is glorious because it has been put to shame. Now, now let us gather the fruits of the bloody sowing. Let us now reap the harvest of the deep ploughing of agony and suffering that our ancestors have endured.

I think that no true-hearted Christian will ever give up any enterprise that God has laid upon him because he fears its ultimate success. "Difficult," said Napoleon, "is not a French word." "Doubtful" is not a Christian word. We are sure to succeed; the gospel must conquer. It is possible for heaven and earth to pass away, but it is not possible for God's Word to fail, and therefore it is utterly impossible that any nation, kindred, or tongue should to the end stand out against the attacks of love, against the invasion of the armies of King Jesus.

Thus, then, you see, a fair argument can be built upon the text. Inasmuch as Christ is to his people a picture of what they are to be, inasmuch as by his suffering all power was given to him in heaven and in earth, so after the sufferings of the church, the wounds of her martyrs, and the deaths of her confessors power shall be given to her in heaven and in earth, and she shall reign with Christ over the nations gloriously.

We now take a second view of the argument. This is the church's right. All power is given to Christ in heaven and in earth. What then? Why, this: Kings and princes, potentates and power, are you aware that your thrones have been given away? Do you know it, you crowned heads, that your crowns have been given— given away from you to one who claims to be King of kings and Lord of lords? Do you pass decrees forbidding the gospel to be preached? We laugh at you! You have no power to prevent it, for all power is given unto Christ in heaven and in earth. Do you say that the missionary has no right upon your shore? The virgin daughter of Zion shakes her head at you, and laughs you to scorn. She has right anywhere and everywhere. She has rights in heaven without limit and rights in earth without bound, for all power is given to her head in heaven and in earth, and she therefore has a patent, a claim that is not to be disputed, to take to herself all countries and all kingdoms, because the power above is given unto Christ.

What is that man doing on yonder shore? He has landed on an island in the South Seas. He is an intruder; banish him at once! Sirs, mind what you do, for surely you fight against God. But the man is sent away, he comes back again, or if not he, another. A severer edict is passed this time, "Let us slay him, that the inheritance may still be ours." But another comes, and another, and another. Why do you stand up and take counsel together against the Lord and against his anointed? These men are not intruders; they are ambassadors come to make peace. Nay, more, they are delegates from heaven come to claim the rightful heritage of King Jesus. You, in putting them away as intruders, have denied the rights of Christ, but to deny is one thing and to disprove another. He has still a right to you, and therefore has the missionary still a right to come wherever he will, preaching the unsearchable riches of Christ.

Once or twice in my life I have met with some miserable little ministers who, when I have gone into a village to preach, have questioned my right to preach in the village because I ought to have asked them first or to have consulted them. And can Christian men look on a district as their own dominion and reckon God's servant as a poacher on their estates or a brigand in their territories? Is there any place on this earth that belongs to any man so that he can shut out God's ministers? We once for all put our foot upon any claim so ridiculous. Wherever there is found a man, there is the minister free to preach. The whole world is our parish; we know of no fetter upon our feet and no gag upon our lips.

Though kings should pass laws, the servants of Christ can bear the penalty, but they cannot disobey their Master. Though the emperor should say the gospel should not be preached by any unauthorized

denomination in France, as I have heard he has said
of late, we care not for him. What cares the church for
a thousand emperors? Their resolutions are mockery,
their laws wastepaper. The church never was yet vassal
to the state or servile slave to principalities and powers, and she neither can nor will be. At all the laws of
states she laughs and utterly defies them, if they come
in the way of the law of Christ that says, "Teach the
gospel to every creature."

Brothers, I say, the church has a right anywhere
and everywhere—a right, not because she tolerated;
the word is insult, not because the law permits; the
law permitting or not permitting, tolerated or untol-
erated, everywhere beneath the arch of God's heaven
God's servants have a right to preach. Oh that they
would claim the right, and in every place teach and
preach Jesus Christ continually!

But now, lastly, it seems to me that the argument
of the text contains the church's might. "All power is
given unto me in heaven and in earth; go, therefore,
and teach all nations, baptizing them in the name of
the Father, and of the Son, and of the Holy Spirit."
You have power to teach; fear not. Let this be your
encouragement: you must succeed, you shall prevail.
There never lived another man save Christ who could
say, "All power is given me on earth." Canute puts his

throne by the side of the sea, but the waves wet his person and prove to his flattering courtiers that he is but a man. What power have kings over the lightning or the rushing winds? Can they control the tides or bid the moon stand still? Power is not given unto man, even upon earth. Much less could any man say that all power in heaven belonged to him. This is a singular expression, one that only could be used by Christ. If any other should attempt to use it, it were an imposition and a blasphemy, but the Lord Jesus Christ can say today, as he said then, "All power is given unto me in heaven and in earth."

Let us think, then, all power is given to Christ in providence. Over common daily events he has supreme authority. You have launched upon the sea, upon a mission voyage—he rules the waves and wings the winds. Fear not, for tempest is his trembling slave. You have come near the shore, but there are hidden reefs and sunken rocks. Fear not, for all power is given to him in the lowest deep to guide you safely and to bring you to your desired haven. A band of men meet you upon the shore, brandishing their weapons. You are unarmed; you have nothing but the Word. You shall now prove that "more is he who is with you than all they who be with them." Go in this your might.

All power is given to Christ—power over the wills of men as well as over the waves of the sea. But political occurrences prevent your landing on a certain country. Through treaties, or a want of treaties, there is no room for the missionary in such-and-such an empire. Pray, and the gates shall be opened. Plead, and the bars of brass shall be cut in twain. Christ has power over politics. He can make wars and create peace with a view to the propagation of his Word. He can change the hearts of princes and preside in the counsels of senates; he can cause nations that have long been shut up to be opened to the truth.

And, indeed, what a wonderful proof we have had of late that all power belongs unto Christ, for human skill has been yoked to the chariot of the gospel. How wondrously, my brothers, have the inventions of man of late years progressed! How could we have preached the gospel to all nations—how could we have even known that America existed—if it had not been that the Lord put it into the mind of Columbus to discover the New World? And how wearisome our life, if with the ordinary slow navigation of the ancient times we had to journey among all nations! But now we are carried across the waves so rapidly that distance is annihilated and time forgotten. Truly God has opened up the world and brought it to our threshold. If he has not made a smaller world, at least he has made it more convenient and nearer to our hand.

And then see how countries, which once could not be reached, have been opened to us. The celestial king of China, the rebel prince, invites us to come and preach. He does not merely permit—he invites. He builds places of worship. He is prepared, he says, that his brothers should come and teach him and all his subjects, for they are imperfectly taught in the things of God. And the imperial sovereign of China too, though he does not invite, permits the missionaries to go among his millions. There is perfect liberty for us to preach to four hundred millions of persons who before had never seen the light of Calvary.

And there is India, too, given up to our dominion, and the old Company, which always impeded us, rolled up in its shroud and laid in its grave. And there are other lands and other places that once seemed environed by impassable mountains into which we have now a road. Oh, for the will to dash through that road riding upon the white horses of salvation! Oh, for the heart, the spirit, and the soul to avail ourselves of the golden opportunity and to preach Christ where he has never been preached before! All power, then, we can clearly see, over everything in this world has been given to Christ and used for the propagation of his truth.

But, brothers, let us recollect that power is given to Christ in heaven as well as on earth. All angels bow before him, and the cherubim and seraphim are ready to obey his high behests. Power is given to him over the plenitude of the Holy Spirit; he can pour out the mysterious energy in such abundance that nations can be born in a day. He can clothe his ministers with salvation and make his priests shout aloud for joy. He has power to intercede with God, and he shall presently send out men to preach, presently give the people the mind to hear, and give the hearers the will to obey.

We have in the midst of us today our Leader. He is not gone from us. If his flesh and blood be absent, yet in body as well as spirit he lives, adorned with the dew and beauty of his youth. As for the Muslim, his leader has long ago rotted in his coffin. But ours lives, and because he lives his truth and his cause live also. We have with us today a Leader whose power is not diminished, whose influence in the highest heavens has suffered no impairing. He is universal Lord. Oh, let our efforts be worthy of the power which he has promised, let our zeal be in some respect akin to his zeal, and let our energy prove that the energy divine has not been withdrawn.

I wish that I could preach this morning, but the more earnestly I feel, the more scant are my words with which to express my emotions. I have prayed to God, and it is a prayer I shall repeat till I die—I have prayed that out of this church there may go many missionaries. I will never be content with a congregation, with a church, or even with ministers, many of whom have already gone out of our midst. We must have missionaries from this church. God's people everywhere will I trust aid me in training young soldiers for my Master's army. God will send the men, and faith will find the means, and we will ourselves send out our own men to proclaim the name of Jesus.

Brothers, it is a singular thing that there some young men get the idea into their minds that they would like to go into foreign lands, but these are frequently the most unfit men and have not the power and ability. Now, I would that the divine call would come to some gifted men. You who have, perhaps, some wealth of your own, what could be a better object in life than to devote yourself and your substance to the Redeemer's cause? You young men who have brilliant prospects before you but do not yet have the anxieties of a family to maintain, why, would it not be a noble thing to surrender your brilliant prospects that you may become a humble preacher of Christ?

The greater the sacrifice, the more honor to yourself and the more acceptable to him.

I have questioned my own conscience, and I do not think I could be in the path of duty if I should go abroad to preach the Word, leaving this field of labor. But I think many of my brothers now laboring at home might with the greatest advantage surrender their charges and leave a land where they would scarce be missed to go where their presence would be as valuable as the presence of a thousand such as they are here. And oh! I long that we may see young men out of the universities and students in our grammar schools—that we may see our physicians, advocates, tradesmen, and educated mechanics, when God has touched their hearts, giving up all they have that they may teach and preach Christ. We want Yanderkists; we want Judsons and Brainerds over again.

It will never do to send out to the heathen men who are of no use at home. We cannot send men of third- and tenth-class abilities; we must send the highest and best. The bravest men must lead the van. O God, anoint your servants, we beseech you; put the fire into their hearts that never can be quenched; make it so hot within their bones that they must die or preach, that they must lie down with broken hearts or else be free to preach where Christ was never heard.

Brothers, I envy any one among you—I say again with truth, I envy you—if it shall be your lot to go to China, the country so lately opened to us. I would gladly change places with you. I would renounce the partial ease of a settlement in this country and renounce the responsibilities of so large a congregation as this with pleasure if I might have your honors. I think sometimes that missionaries in the field—if it be right to compare great things with such small ones—might say to you, as our English king did to his soldiers at the battle of Agineourt, changing the word for a moment:

> Ministers in England, now a bed,
> Might think themselves accurs'd they
>   were not here,
> And hold their manhood's cheap, while
>   any speak
> Who fought with us upon this glorious
>   day.

Have we none out of our sixteen hundred members—have we none out of this congregation of six thousand—who can say, "Here am I, send me"? Jesus! Is there not one? Must heathens perish? Must the gods of the heathen hold their thrones? Must your kingdom fail? Are there none to own you, none to maintain your righteous cause? If there be none, let us weep, each one of us, because such a calamity has fallen on us. But if there be any who are willing to give all for Christ, let us who are compelled to stay at home do our best to help them. Let us see to it that they lack nothing, for we cannot send them out without purse or scrip. Let us fill the purse of the men whose hearts God has filled and take care of them temporally, leaving it for God to preserve them spiritually.

May the Lord, the Divine Master, add his blessing to the feeble words that I have uttered, and let me not conclude till I have said, I must teach you too, and this is the teaching of God—"Believe in the Lord Jesus Christ and you shall be saved." Trust him with your soul, and he will save you. For "He that believes and is baptized shall be saved; he that believes not shall be damned."

How to Become Fishers of Men[3]

"And he saith unto them, Follow me,
and I will make you fishers of men."
(Matthew 4:19)

When Christ calls us by his grace, we ought not only to remember what we are, but we ought also to think of what he can make us. It is "Follow me, and I will make you." We should repent of what we have been but rejoice in what we may be. It is not "Follow me because of what you are already." It

---

3. Published in *Metropolitan Tabernacle Pulpit*, Vol. 32 in 1886 by Charles Spurgeon. This is sermon 1906, delivered in 1886, exact date unknown.

is not "Follow me because you may make something of yourselves" but, "Follow me because of what I will make you."

Verily, I might say of each one of us as soon as we are converted, "It does not yet appear what we shall be." It did not seem a likely thing that lowly fishermen would develop into apostles, that men so handy with the net would be quite as much at home in preaching sermons and in instructing converts. One would have said, "How can these things be? You cannot make founders of churches out of peasants of Galilee." That is exactly what Christ did, and when we are brought low in the sight of God by a sense of our own unworthiness, we may feel encouraged to follow Jesus because of what he can make us.

What said the woman of a sorrowful spirit when she lifted up her song? "He raises up the poor out of the dust, and lifts up the beggar from the dunghill, to set them among princes." We cannot tell what God may make of us in the new creation, since it would have been quite impossible to have foretold what he made of chaos in the old creation. Who could have imagined all the beautiful things that came forth from darkness and disorder by that one fiat, "Let there be light"? And who can tell what lovely displays of everything that is divinely fair may yet appear in a man's formerly dark life when God's grace has said to him, "Let there be light"? O you who see in yourselves at present nothing that is desirable, come you and follow Christ for the sake of what he can make out of you. Do you not hear his sweet voice calling to you, and saying, "Follow me, and I will make you fishers of men"?

Note, next, that we are not made all that we shall be, nor all that we ought to desire to be, when we are ourselves fished for and caught. This is what the grace of God does for us at first, but it is not all. We are like the fishes, making sin to be our element; and the good Lord comes, and with the gospel net he takes us, and he delivers us from the life and love of sin. But he has not wrought for us all that he can do, nor all that we should wish him to do, when he has done this. For it is another and a higher miracle to make us who were fish to become fishers—to make the saved ones saviors, to make the convert into a converter, the receiver of the gospel into an imparter of that same gospel to other people.

I think I may say to every person whom I am addressing: If you are saved yourself, the work is but half done until you are employed to bring others to Christ. You are as yet but half formed in the image of your Lord. You have not attained to the full development of the Christ-life in you unless you have commenced in some feeble way to tell others of the grace of God, and I trust that you will find no rest to the sole of your foot till you have been the means of leading many to that blessed Savior who is your confidence and your hope. His word is, "Follow me, not merely that you may be saved, nor even that you may be sanctified,: but, "Follow me, and I will make you fishers of men." Be following Christ with that intent and aim, and fear that you are not perfectly following him unless in some degree he is making use of you to be fishers of men.

The fact is that every one of us must take to the business of a mancatcher. If Christ has caught us, we must catch others. If we have been apprehended of him, we must be his constables to apprehend rebels for him. Let us ask him to give us grace to go fishing and so to cast our nets that we may take a great multitude of fishes. Oh that the Holy Spirit may raise up from among us some master fishers who shall sail their boats in many a sea and surround great shoals of fish!

My teaching at this time will be very simple, but I hope it will be eminently practical, for my longing is that not one of you that love the Lord may be backward in his service. What says the Song of Solomon concerning certain sheep that come up from the washing? It says, "Every one bears twins, and none is barren among them." May that be so with all the members of this church and all the Christian people who hear or read this sermon!

The fact is, the day is very dark. The heavens are lowering with heavy thunderclouds. Men little dream of what tempests may soon shake this city—and the whole social fabric of this land—even to a general breaking up of society. So dark may the night become that the stars may seem to fall like blighted fruit from the tree. The times are evil. Now, if never before, every glowworm must show its spark. You with the tiniest farthing candle must take it from under the bushel and set it on a candlestick. There is need of you all.

Lot was a poor creature. He was a very, very wretched kind of believer, but still he might have been a great blessing to Sodom had he but pleaded for it as he should have done. And poor, poor Christians, as I fear many are, one begins to value every truly converted soul in these evil days and to pray that each one may glorify the Lord. I pray that every righteous man, vexed as he is with the conversation of the wicked, may be more importunate in prayer than he has ever been, return unto his God, and get more spiritual life that he may be a blessing to the perishing people around him. I address you, therefore, at this time first of all upon this thought. Oh that the Spirit of God may make each one of you feel his personal responsibility!

Here is for believers in Christ, in order to their usefulness, something for them to do. "Follow me." But, secondly, here is something to be done by their great Lord and Master: "Follow me, and I will make you fishers of men." You will not grow into fishers of yourselves, but this is what Jesus will do for you if you will but follow him. And then, lastly, here is a good illustration, used according to our great Master's wont; for scarcely without a parable did he speak unto the people. He presents us with an illustration of what Christian men should be—fishers of men. We may get some useful hints out of it, and I pray the Holy Spirit to bless them to us.

What the Christian Does

First, then, I will take it for granted that every believer here wants to be useful. If he does not, I take leave to question whether he can be a true believer in Christ. Well, then, if you want to be really useful, here is something for you to do to that end: "Follow me, and I will make you fishers of men."

What is the way to become an efficient preacher? "Young man," says one, "go to college." "Young man," says Christ, "follow me, and I will make you a fisher of men." How is a person to be useful? "Attend a training class," says one. Quite right, but there is a surer answer than that—Follow Jesus, and he will make you fishers of men. The great training school for Christian workers has Christ at its head, and he is at its head not only as a tutor but as a leader. We are not only to learn of him in study but to follow him in action. "Follow me, and I will make you fishers of men."

The direction is very distinct and plain, and I believe that it is exclusive so that no man can become a fisherman by any other process. This process may appear to be very simple, but assuredly it is most efficient. The Lord Jesus Christ, who knew all about fishing for men, was himself the Dictator of the rule, "Follow me, if you want to be fishers of men. If you would be useful, keep in my track."

I understand this, first, in this sense: he separates unto Christ. These men were to leave their pursuits. They were to leave their companions. They were, in fact, to quit the world, that their one business might be, in their Master's name, to be fishers of men. We are not all called to leave our daily business or to quit our families. That might be rather running away from the fishery than working at it in God's name. But we are called most distinctly to come out from among the ungodly, to be separate, and not to touch the unclean thing. We cannot be fishers of men if we remain among men in the same element with them. Fish will not be fishers. The sinner will not convert the sinner. The ungodly man will not convert the ungodly man, and what is more to the point, the worldly Christian will not convert the world. If you are of the world, no doubt the world will love its own, but you cannot save the world. If you are dark and belong to the kingdom of darkness, you cannot remove the darkness. If you march with the armies of the wicked one, you cannot defeat them.

I believe that one reason why the church of God at this present moment has so little influence over the world is because the world has so much influence over the church. Nowadays we hear Nonconformists pleading that they may do this and they may do that— things that their Puritan forefathers would rather have died at the stake than have tolerated. They plead that they may live like worldlings, and my sad answer to them, when they crave for this liberty, is, "Do it if you dare. It may not do you much hurt, for you are so bad already. Your cravings show how rotten your hearts are. If you have a hungering after such dog's meat, go, dogs, and eat the garbage.

Worldly amusements are fit food for mere pretenders and hypocrites. If you were God's children you would loathe the very thought of the world's evil joys, and your question would not be, "How far may we be like the world?" but your one cry would be, "How far can we get away from the world? How much can we come out from it?" Your temptation would be rather to become sternly severe and ultra-puritanical in your separation from sin, in such a time as this, than to ask, "How can I make myself like other men, and act as they do?"

Brothers, the use of the church in the world is that it should be like salt in the midst of putrefaction, but if the salt has lost its savor, what is the good of it? If it were possible for salt itself to putrefy, it could but be an increase and a heightening of the general putridity. The worst day the world ever saw was when the sons of God were joined with the daughters of men. Then came the flood, for the only barrier against a flood of vengeance on this world is the separation of the saint from the sinner. Your duty as a Christian is to stand fast in your own place and stand out for God, hating even the garment spotted by the flesh, resolving like one of old that, let others do as they will, as for you and your house, you will serve the Lord.

Come, you children of God, you must stand out with your Lord outside the camp. Jesus calls to you today and says, "Follow me." Was Jesus found at the theater? Did he frequent the sports of the racecourse? Was Jesus seen, think you, in any of the amusements of the Herodian court? Not he. He was "holy, harmless, undefiled, and separate from sinners." In one sense, no one mixed with sinners so completely as he did when, like a physician, he went among them healing bis patients. But in another sense there was a gulf fixed between the men of the world and the Savior that he never assayed to cross and that they could not cross to defile him. The first lesson the church has to learn is this: Follow Jesus into the separated state, and he will make you fishers of men. Unless you take up your cross and protest against an ungodly world, you cannot hope that the holy Jesus will make you fishers of men.

A second meaning of our text is very obviously this: abide with Christ, and then you will be made fishers of men. These disciples whom Christ called were to come and live with him. They were every day to be associated with him. They were to hear him teach publicly the everlasting gospel, and in addition they were to receive choice explanations in private of the word he had spoken. They were to be his body servants and his familiar friends. They were to see his miracles and hear his prayers, and better still, they were to be with himself and become one with him in his holy labor. It was given to them to sit at the table with him and even to have their feet washed by him. Many of them fulfilled that word, "Where you dwell, I will dwell." They were with him in his afflictions and persecutions. They witnessed his secret agonies; they saw his many tears; they marked the passion and the compassion of his soul, and thus, after their measure, they caught his spirit, and so they learned to be fishers of men.

At Jesus's feet we must learn the art and mystery of soul winning: to live with Christ is the best education for usefulness. It is a great boon to any man to be associated with a Christian minister whose heart is on fire. The best training for a young man is that which the Vaudois pastors were wont to give, when each old man had a young man with him who walked with him whenever he went up the mountainside to preach, lived in the house with him, and marked his prayers and saw his daily piety. This was a fine instruction, was it not? But it will not compare with that of the apostles who lived with Jesus himself and were his daily companions. Matchless was the training of the twelve. No wonder that they became what they were with such a heavenly tutor to saturate them with his own spirit!

And now today his bodily presence is not among us, but his spiritual power is perhaps more fully known to us than it was to those apostles in those two or three years of the Lord's corporeal presence. There are some of us to whom he is intimately near. We know more about him than we do about our dearest earthly friend. We have never been able quite to read our friend's heart in all its twistings and windings, but we know the heart of the Well Beloved. We have leaned our head upon his bosom and have enjoyed fellowship with him such as we could not have with any of our own kith and kin. This is the surest method of learning how to do good. Live with Jesus, follow Jesus, and he will make you fishers of men. See how he does the work, and so learn how to do it yourself. A Christian man should be bound apprentice to Jesus to learn the trade of a Savior. We can never save men by offering a redemption, for we have none to present; but we can learn how to save men by warning them to flee from the wrath to come, and setting before them the one great effectual remedy. See how Jesus saves, and you will learn how the thing is done. There is no learning it anyhow else. Live in fellowship with Christ, and there shall be about you an air and a manner as of one who has been made in heart and mind apt to teach and wise to win souls.

A third meaning, however, must be given to this "Follow me," and it is this: "Obey me, and then you shall know what to do to save men." We must not talk about our fellowship with Christ or our being separated from the world unto him unless we make him our Master and Lord in everything. Some public teachers are not true at all points to their convictions, and how can they look for a blessing? A Christian man anxious to be useful ought to be very particular as to every point of obedience to his Master.

I have no doubt whatever that God blesses our churches even when they are very faulty, for his mercy endures forever. When there is a measure of error in the teaching and a measure of mistake in the practice, he may still vouchsafe to use the ministry, for he is very gracious. But a large measure of blessing must necessarily be withheld from all teaching that is knowingly or glaringly faulty. God can set his seal upon the truth that is in it, but he cannot set his seal upon the error that is in it. Out of mistakes about Christian ordinances and other things, especially errors in heart and spirit, there may come evils that we never looked for.

Such evils may even now be telling upon the present age and may work worse mischief upon future generations.

If we desire as fishers of men to be largely used of God, we must copy our Lord Jesus in everything and obey him in every point. Failure in obedience may lead to failure in success. Each one of us, if he would wish to see his child saved, his Sunday school class blessed, or his congregation converted, must take care that, bearing the vessels of the Lord, he is himself clean. Anything we do that grieves the Spirit of God must take away from us some part of our power for good. The Lord is very gracious and pitiful, but yet he is a jealous God. He is sometimes sternly jealous toward his people who are living in neglects of known duty or in associations that are not clean in his sight. He will wither their work, weaken their strength, and humble them until at last they say, "My Lord, I will take your way after all. I will do what you bid me to do, for else thou wilt not accept me."

The Lord said to his disciples, "Go into all the world and preach the gospel to every creature; he that believes and is baptized shall be saved." And he promised them that signs should follow, and so they did follow them, and so they will. But we must get back to apostolic practice and to apostolic teaching. We must

lay aside the commandments of men and the whim-
seys of our own brains, and we must do what Christ
tells us, as Christ tells us, and because Christ tells us.
Definitely and distinctly, we must take the place of
servants, and if we will not do that, we cannot expect
our Lord to work with us and by us. Let us be determined that, as true as the needle is to the pole, so true
will we be, as far as our light goes, to the command
of our Lord and Master. Jesus says, "Follow me, and
I will make you fishers of men." By this teaching he
seems to say—"Go beyond me, or fall back behind
me, and you may cast the net, but it shall be night with
you, and that night you shall take nothing. When you
shall do as I bid you, you shall cast your net on the
right side of the ship, and you shall find."

Again, I think that there is a great lesson in my
text to those who preach their own thoughts instead
of preaching the thoughts of Christ. These disciples
were to follow Christ that they might listen to him,
hear what he had to say, drink in his teaching, and
then go and teach what he had taught them. Their
Lord says, "What I tell you in darkness, speak in light.
And what you hear in the ear, preach upon the house-
tops." If they will be faithful reporters of Christ's message, he will make them "fishers of men."

But you know the boastful method nowadays is this: "I am not going to preach this old, old gospel, this musty Puritan doctrine. I will sit down in my study, burn the midnight oil, and invent a new theory. Then I will come out with my brand-new thought and blaze away with it." Many are not following Christ but following themselves, and of them the Lord may well say, "You shall see whose word shall stand, mine or theirs." Others are wickedly prudent and judge that certain truths that are evidently God's Word had better be kept back. You must not be rough but must prophesy smooth things. To talk about the punishment of sin, to speak of eternal punishment, why, these are unfashionable doctrines. It may be that they are taught in the Word of God, but they do not suit the genius of the age. We must pare them down.

Brothers in Christ, I will have no share in this. Will you? O my soul, come not into their secret! Certain things not taught in the Bible our enlightened age has discovered. Evolution may be clean contrary to the teaching of Genesis, but that does not matter. We are not going to be believers of Scripture, but original thinkers. This is the vainglorious ambition of the period. Mark you, in proportion as the modern theology is preached the vice of this generation increases.

To a great degree I attribute the looseness of the age to the laxity of the doctrine preached by its teachers.

From the pulpit they have taught the people that sin is a trifle. From the pulpit these traitors to God and to his Christ have taught the people that there is no hell to be feared. A little, little hell, perhaps there may be, but just punishment for sin is made nothing of. The precious atoning sacrifice of Christ has been derided and misrepresented by those who were pledged to preach it. They have given the people the name of the gospel, but the gospel itself has evaporated in their hands. From hundreds of pulpits the gospel is as clean gone as the dodo from its old haunts, and still the preachers take the position and name of Christ's ministers. Well, and what comes of it? Why, their congregations grow thinner and thinner, and so it must be.

Jesus says, "Follow me, I will make you fishers of men," but if you go in your own way, with your own net, you will make nothing of it, and the Lord promises you no help in it. The Lord's directions make himself our leader and example. It is, "Follow me, follow me. Preach my gospel. Preach what I preached. Teach what I taught, and keep to that." With that blessed servility that becomes one whose ambition it is to be a copyist and never to be an original, copy

Christ even in jots and tittles. Do this, and he will make you fishers of men, but if you do not do this, you shall fish in vain.

I close this head of discourse by saying that we shall not be fishers of men unless we follow Christ in one other respect; and that is, by endeavoring in all points to imitate his holiness. Holiness is the most real power that can be possessed by men or women. We may preach orthodoxy, but we must also live orthodoxy. God forbid that we should preach anything else, but it will be all in vain unless there is a life at the back of the testimony. An unholy preacher may even render truth contemptible. In proportion as any of us draw back from a living and zealous sanctification, we shall draw back from the place of power. Our power lies in this word, "Follow me." Be Jesus-like. In all things endeavor to think, speak, and act as Jesus did, and he will make you fishers of men.

This will require self-denial. We must daily take up the cross. This may require willingness to give up our reputation—readiness to be thought fools, idiots, and the like, as men are apt to call those who are keeping close to their Master. There must be the cheerful resigning of everything that looks like honor and personal glory, in order that we may be wholly Christ's, and glorify his name. We must live his life and be ready to die his death, if need be. O brothers, sisters, if we do this and follow Jesus, putting our feet into the footprints of his pierced feet, he will make us fishers of men. If it should so please him that we should even die without having gathered many souls to the cross, we shall speak from our graves. In some way or other the Lord will make a holy life to be an influential life. It is not possible that a life that can be described as a following of Christ should be an unsuccessful one in the sight of the Most High. "Follow me," and there is an "I will" such as God can never draw back from: "Follow me, and I will make you fishers of men."

Thus much on the first point. There is something for us to do: we are graciously called to follow Jesus. Holy Spirit, lead us to do it.

What the Lord Does

But secondly, and briefly, there is something for the Lord to do. When his dear servants are following him, he says, "I will make you fishers of men." And be it never forgotten that it is he who makes us follow him, so that if the following of him is the step to being made a fisher of men, yet this he gives us. 'Tis all of his Spirit. I have talked about catching his spirit, abiding in him, obeying him, hearkening to him, and copying him, but none of these things are we capable of apart from his working them all in us. "From me is your fruit found," is a text that we must not for a moment forget. So, then, if we do follow him, it is he who makes us follow him; and so he makes us fishers of men.

But, further, if we follow Christ he will make us fishers of men by all our experience. I am sure that the man who is really consecrated to bless others will be helped in this by all that he feels, especially by his afflictions. I often feel very grateful to God that I have undergone fearful depression of spirits. I know the borders despair and the horrible brink of that gulf of darkness into which my feet have almost gone, but hundreds of times I have been able to give a helpful grip to brothers and sisters who have come into that same condition, which grip I could never have given if I had not known their deep despondency. So I believe that the darkest and most dreadful experience of a child of God will help him to be a fisher of men if he will but follow Christ. Keep close to your Lord and he will make every step a blessing to you.

If God in providence should make you rich, he will fit you to speak to those ignorant and wicked rich who so much abound in this city and so often are the cause of its worst sin. And if the Lord is pleased to let you be very poor, you can go down and talk to those wicked and ignorant poor people who so often are the cause of sin in this city and so greatly need the gospel. The winds of providence will waft you where you can fish for men. The wheels of providence are full of eyes, and all those eyes will look this way to help us to be winners of souls. You will often be surprised to find how God has been in a house that you visit; before you get there, his hand has been at work in its chambers. When you wish to speak to some particular individual, God's providence has been dealing with that individual to make him ready for just that word you could say but nobody else but you could say. Oh, be you following Christ, and you will find that he will, by every experience through which you are passing, make you fishers of men.

Further than that, if you will follow him he will make you fishers of men by distinct warnings in your own heart. There are many warnings from God's Spirit that are not noticed by Christians when they are in a callous condition, but when the heart is right with God and living in communion with God, we feel a sacred sensitiveness, so that we do not need the Lord to shout, but his faintest whisper is heard. Nay, he need not even whisper. "You shall guide me with your eye." Oh, how many mulish Christians there are who must be held in with bit and bridle and receive a cut of the whip every now and then! But the Christian who follows his Lord shall be tenderly guided.

I do not say that the Spirit of God will say to you, "Go and join yourself unto this chariot," or that you will hear a word in your ear. But yet in your soul, as distinctly as the Spirit said to Philip, "Go and join yourself to this chariot," you shall hear the Lord's will. As soon as you see an individual, the thought shall cross your mind, "Go and speak to that person." Every opportunity of usefulness shall be a call to you. If you are ready, the door shall open before you, and you shall hear a voice behind you saying, "This is the way; walk in it." If you have the grace to run in the right way, you shall never be long without an intimation as to what the right way is. That right way shall lead you to river or sea, where you can cast your net and be a fisher of men.

Then, too, I believe that the Lord meant by this that he would give his followers the Holy Spirit. They were to follow him, and then, when they had seen him ascend into the holy place of the Most High, they were to tarry at Jerusalem for a little while and the Spirit would come upon them and clothe them with a mysterious power. This word was spoken to Peter and Andrew, and you know how it was fulfilled to

Peter. What a host of fish he brought to land the first time he cast the net in the power of the Holy Spirit! "Follow me, and I will make you fishers of men."

Brothers, we have no conception of what God could do by this company of believers gathered in the Tabernacle tonight. If now we were to be filled with the Holy Spirit, there are enough of us to evangelize London. There are enough here to be the means of the salvation of the world. God saves not by many nor by few.

Let us seek a benediction; and if we seek it let us hear this directing voice, "Follow me, and I will make you fishers of men." You men and women who sit before me, you are by the shore of a great sea of human life swarming with the souls of men. You live in the midst of millions, but if you will follow Jesus and be faithful to him, true to him, and do what he bids you, he will make you fishers of men.

Do not say, "Who shall save this city?" The weakest shall be strong enough. Gideon's barley cake shall smite the tent and make it lay along. Samson, with the jawbone taken up from the earth where it was lying bleaching in the sun, shall smite the Philistines. Fear not, neither be dismayed. Let your responsibilities drive you closer to your Master. Let horror of prevailing sin make you look into his dear face who long ago wept over Jerusalem and now weeps over London. Clasp him, and never let go your hold. By the strong and mighty impulses of the divine life within you, quickened and brought to maturity by the Spirit of God, learn this lesson from your Lord's own mouth: "Follow me, and I will make you fishers of men." You are not fit for it, but he will make you fit. You cannot do it of yourselves, but he will make you do it. You do not know how to spread nets and draw shoals of fish to shore, but he will teach you. Only follow him, and he will make you fishers of men.

I wish that I could somehow say this as with a voice of thunder, that the whole church of God might hear it. I wish I could write it in stars athwart the sky, Jesus says, "Follow me, and I will make you fishers of men." If you forget the precept, the promise shall never be yours. If you follow some other track or imitate some other leader, you shall fish in vain. God grant us to believe fully that Jesus can do great things in us, and then do great things by us for the good of our fellows!

An Illustration

The last point you might work out in full for yourselves in your private meditations with much profit. We have here a figure full of instruction. I will give you but two or three thoughts you can use. "I will make you fishers of men." You have been fishers of fish; if you follow me, I will make you fishers of men.

A fisher is a person who is very dependent and needs to be trustful. He cannot see the fish. One who fishes in the sea must go and cast in the neb, as it were, at a peradventure. Fishing is an act of faith. I have often seen in the Mediterranean men go with their boats and enclose acres of sea with vast nets, and yet, when they have drawn the net to shore, they have not had as much result as I could put in my hand. A few wretched silvery nothings have made up the whole take. Yet they have gone again and cast the great neb several times a day, hopefully expecting something to come of it.

Nobody is so dependent upon God as the minister of God. Oh, this fishing from the Tabernacle pulpit! What a work of faith! I cannot tell that a soul will be brought to God by it. I cannot judge whether my sermon will be suitable to the persons who are here, except that I do believe that God will guide me in the casting of the net. I expect him to work salvation, and I depend upon him for it. I love this complete dependence, and if I could be offered a certain amount of preaching power by which I could save sinners, which should be entirely at my own disposal, I would beg the Lord not to let me have it, for it is far more delightful to be entirely dependent upon him at all times. It is good to be a fool when Christ is made unto you wisdom. It is a blessed thing to be weak if Christ becomes more fully your strength. Go to work, you who would be fishers of men, and yet feel your insufficiency. You who have no strength, attempt this divine work. Your Master's strength will be seen when your own has all gone. A fisherman is a dependent person; he must look up for success every time he puts the net down, but still he is a trustful person, and therefore he casts in the net joyfully.

A fisherman who gets his living by it is a diligent and persevering man. The fishers are up at dawn. At daybreak our fishermen off the Doggerbank are fishing, and they continue fishing till late in the afternoon. As long as hands can work, men will fish. May the Lord Jesus make us hardworking, persevering, unwearied fishers of men! "In the morning sow your seed, and in the evening withhold not your hand; for you know not whether shall prosper, either this or that."

The fisherman in his own craft is intelligent and watchful. It looks very easy, I dare say, to be a fisherman, but you would find that it was no child's play if you were to take a real part in it. There is an art in it, from the mending of the net right on to the pulling it to shore. How diligent the fisherman is to prevent the fish leaping out of the net! I heard a great noise one night in the sea, as if some huge drum were being beaten by a giant, and I looked out, and I saw that the fishermen of Mentone were beating the water to drive the fish into the net, or to keep them from leaping out when they had once encompassed them with it. Ah, yes! And you and I will often have to be watching the corners of the gospel net lest sinners who are almost caught should make their escape. They are very crafty, these fish, and they use this craftiness in endeavoring to avoid salvation. We shall have to be always at our business and to exercise all our wits, and more than our own wits, if we are to be successful fishers of men.

The fisherman is a very laborious person. It is not at all an easy calling. He does not sit in an armchair and catch fish. He has to go out in rough weathers. If he who regards the clouds will not sow, I am sure that he who regards the clouds will never fish. If we never do any work for Christ except when we feel up to the mark, we shall not do much. If we feel that we will not pray because we cannot pray, we shall never pray. And if we say, "I will not preach today because I do not feel that I could preach," we shall never preach any preaching that is worth the preaching. We must be always at it, until we wear ourselves out, throwing our whole soul into the work in all weathers for Christ's sake.

The fisherman is a daring man. He tempts the boisterous sea. A little brine in his face does not hurt him; he has been wet through a thousand times; it is nothing to him. He never expected when he became a deep-sea fisherman that he was going to sleep in the lap of ease. So the true minister of Christ who fishes for souls will never mind a little risk. He will be bound to do or say many a thing that is very unpopular, and some Christian people may even judge his utterances to be too severe. He must do and say that which is for the good of souls. It is not his to entertain a question as to what others will think of his doctrine or of him, but in the name of the Almighty God he must feel, "If the sea roar and the fullness thereof, still at my Master's command I will let down the net."

Now, in the last place, the man whom Christ makes a fisher of men is successful. "But," says one, "I have always heard that Christ's ministers are to be faithful, but that they cannot be sure of being successful." Yes, I have heard that saying, and one way I know it is true, but another way I have my doubts about it. He that is faithful is, in God's way and in God's judgment, successful, more or less.

For instance, here is a brother who says that he is faithful. Of course, I must believe him, yet I never heard of a sinner being saved under him. Indeed, I should think that the safest place for a person to be in if he did not want to be saved would be under this gentleman's ministry because he does not preach anything that is likely to arouse, impress, or convince anybody. This brother is "faithful," so he says. Well, if any person in the world said to you, "I am a fisherman, but I have never caught anything," you would wonder how he could be called a fisherman. A farmer who never grew any wheat, or any other crop—is he a farmer?

When Jesus Christ says, "Follow me, and I will make you fishers of men," he means that you shall really catch men—that you really shall save some. For he who never did get any fish is not a fisherman. He who never saved a sinner after years of work is not a minister of Christ. If the result of his lifework is nil, he made a mistake when he undertook it. Go with the fire of God in your hand and fling it among the stubble, and the stubble will burn. Be sure of that. Go and scatter the good seed: it may not all fall in fruitful places, but some of it will. Be sure of that. Do but shine, and some eye or other will be lightened thereby. You must, you shall succeed. But remember this is the Lord's word—"Follow me, and I will make you fishers of men." Keep close to Jesus, and do as Jesus did, in his spirit, and he will make you fishers of men.

Perhaps I speak to an attentive hearer who is not converted at all. Friend, I have the same thing to say to you. You also may follow Christ, and then he can use you, even you. I do not know but that he has brought you to this place that you may be saved, and that in after years he may make you speak for his name and glory. Remember how he called Saul of Tarsus and made him the apostle of the Gentiles. Reclaimed poachers make the best gamekeepers, and saved sinners make the ablest preachers. Oh, that you would run away from your old master tonight without giving him a minute's notice, for if you give him any notice, he will hold you. Hasten to Jesus, and say, "Here is a poor runaway slave! My Lord, I bear the fetters still upon my wrists. Wilt thou set me free, and make me thine own?" Remember, it is written, "He who comes to me I will in no wise cast out." Never a runaway slave came to Christ in the middle of the night without his taking him in, and he never gave one up to his old master. If Jesus makes you free, you shall be free indeed. Flee away to Jesus, then, on a sudden. May his good Spirit help you, and he will by-and-by make you a winner of others to his praise! God bless you. Amen.

Christ's First and
Last Subject[4]

"From that time Jesus began to preach, and to say,
Repent: for the kingdom of heaven is at hand."
(Matthew 4:17)

"And that repentance and remission of sins
should be preached in his name among
all nations, beginning at Jerusalem."
(Luke 24:47)

I t seems from these two texts that repentance was
the first subject upon which the Redeemer dwelt,

---

4. Published in *Metropolitan Tabernacle Pulpit*, Vol. 6 in 1880
by Charles Spurgeon. This is sermon 329, delivered on August
19, 1860.

and that it was the last that, with his departing breath, he commended to the earnestness of his disciples. He begins his mission crying, "Repent!" He ends it by saying to his successors the apostles, "Preach repentance and remission of sins among all nations, beginning at Jerusalem." This seems to me to be a very interesting fact, and not simply interesting but instructive.

Jesus Christ opens his commission by preaching repentance. What then? Did he not by this act teach us how important repentance was—so important that the very first time he opens his mouth, he begins with, "Repent, for the kingdom of heaven is at hand." Did he not feel that repentance was necessary to be preached before he preached faith in himself, because the soul must first repent of sin before it will seek a Savior or even care to know whether there is a Savior at all? And did he not also indicate to us that as repentance was the opening lesson of the divine teaching, so, if we would be his disciples, we must begin by sitting on the stool of repentance before we can possibly go upward to the higher forms of faith and of full assurance?

Jesus at the first begins with repentance—that repentance may be the Alpha, the first letter of the spiritual alphabet that all believers must learn. And when he concluded his divine commission with repentance, what did he say to us but this—that repentance was still of the very last importance? He preaches it with his first, and he will utter it with his last breath; with this he begins, and with this he will conclude. He knew that repentance was to spiritual life a sort of Alpha and Omega—the duty of the beginning an d the duty of the end. He seemed to say to us, "Repentance, which I preached to you three years ago when I first came into the world as a public teacher, is as binding, as necessary for you who heard me then and who then obeyed my voice as it was at the very first instant. And it is equally needful that you who have been with me from the beginning should not imagine that the theme is exhausted and out of date. You too must begin your ministry and conclude it with the same exhortation, 'Repent and be converted, for the kingdom of heaven is at hand.'"

It seems to me that nothing could set forth Jesus Christ's idea of the high value of repentance more fully and effectually than the fact that he begins with it and concludes with it, that he should say, "Repent," as the keynote of his ministry, preaching this duty before he fully develops all the mystery of godliness, and that he should close his life song as a good composer must, with his first keynote, bidding his disciples still cry, "Repentance and remission of sins are preached in Jesus's name."

I feel then that I need no further apology for introducing to your solemn and serious attention the subject of saving repentance. And oh! While we are talking of it, may God the Holy Spirit breathe into all our spirits, and may we now repent before him and now find those blessings that he has promised to the penitent.

With regard to repentance, these four things: first, its origin; secondly, its essentials; thirdly, its companions; and fourthly, its excellencies.

The Origin of Repentance

When we cry, "Repent and be converted," there are some foolish men who call us legal. Now we beg to state, at the opening of this first point, that repentance is of gospel parentage. It was not born near Mount Sinai. It never was brought forth anywhere but upon Mount Zion. Of course, repentance is a duty—a natural duty—because when man has sinned, who is brazen enough to say that it is not man's bounden duty to repent of having done so? It is a duty that even nature itself would teach.

But gospel repentance was never yet produced as a matter of duty. It was never brought forth in the soul by demands of law, nor indeed can the law, except as the instrument in the hand of grace, even assist the soul toward saving repentance. It is a remarkable fact that the law itself makes no provision for repentance. It says, "This do, and you shall live; break my command, and you shall die." There is nothing said about penitence; there is no offer of pardon made to those that repent. The law pronounces its deadly curse upon the man that sins but once, but it offers no way of escape, no door by which the man may be restored to favor. The barren sides of Sinai have no soil in which to nourish the lovely plant of penitence. Upon Sinai the dew of mercy never fell. Its lightnings and its thunders have frightened away the angel of mercy once for all, and there Justice sits, with sword of flame, upon its majestic throne of rugged rock, never purposing for a moment to put up its sword into the scabbard and to forgive the offender.

Read attentively the twentieth chapter of Exodus. You have the commandments there all thundered forth with trumpet voice, but there is no pause between where Mercy with her silver voice may step in and say, "But if you break this law, God will have mercy upon you and will show himself gracious if you repent." No words of repentance, I say, were ever proclaimed by the law, no promise by it made to penitents; and no assistance is by the law ever offered to those who desire to be forgiven.

Repentance is a gospel grace. Christ preached it, but not Moses. Moses neither can nor will assist a soul to repent; only Jesus can use the law as a means of conviction and an argument for repentance. Jesus gives pardon to those who seek it with weeping and with tears, but Moses knows of no such thing. If repentance is ever obtained by the poor sinner, it must be found at the foot of the cross and not where the Ten Commandments lie shivered at Sinai's base.

And as repentance is of gospel parentage, I make a second remark: it is also of gracious origin. Repentance was never yet produced in any man's heart apart from the grace of God. As soon may you expect the leopard to regret the blood with which its fangs are moistened, as soon might you expect the lion of the wood to abjure his cruel tyranny over the feeble beasts of the plain, as expect the sinner to make any confession or offer any repentance that shall be accepted of God unless grace shall first renew the heart. Go and loose the bands of everlasting winter in the frozen north with your own feeble breath and then hope to make tears of penitence bedew the cheek of the hardened sinner. Go and divide the earth and pierce its bowels with an infant's finger and then hope that your eloquent appeal, unassisted by divine grace, shall be able to penetrate the adamantine heart of man.

Man can sin, and he can continue in it, but to leave the hateful element is a work for which he needs a power divine. As the river rushes downward with increasing fury, leaping from crag to crag in ponderous cataracts of power, so is the sinner in his sin: onward and downward, onward, yet more swiftly, more mightily, more irresistibly in his hellish course. Nothing but divine grace can bid that cataract leap upward or make the floods retrace the pathway they have worn for themselves down the rocks. Nothing, I say, but the power that made the world and dug the foundations of the great deep can ever make the heart of man a fountain of life from which the floods of repentance may gush forth.

So then, soul, if you shalt ever repent, it must be a repentance not of nature but of grace. Nature can imitate repentance; it can produce remorse; it can generate the feeble resolve; it can even lead to a partial, practical reform. But unaided nature cannot touch the vitals and newly create the soul. Nature may make the eyes weep, but it cannot make the heart bleed. Nature can bid you amend your ways, but it cannot renew your heart. No, you must look upward, sinner. You must look upward to him who is able to save unto the uttermost. You must at his hands receive the meek and tender spirit. From his finger must come the touch that shall dissolve the rock, and from his eye must dart the flash of love and light that can scatter the darkness of your impenitence. Remember, then, at the outset, that true repentance is of gospel origin and is not the work of the law; and on the other hand, it is of gracious origin and is not the work of the creature.

The Essentials of Repentance

But to pass forward from this first point to our second head, let us notice the essentials of true repentance. The old divines adopted various methods of explaining penitence. Some of them said it was a precious medicine compounded of six things, but in looking over their divisions I have felt that I might with equal success divide repentance into four different ingredients. This precious box of ointment that must be broken over the Savior's heard before the sweet perfume of peace can ever be smelt in the soul—this precious ointment is compounded of four most rare, most costly things. God give them to us and then give us the compound itself mixed by the Master's hand. True repentance consists of illumination, humiliation, detestation, and transformation.

To take them one by one. The first part of true repentance consists of illumination. Man by nature is impenitent because he does not know himself to be guilty. There are many acts he commits in which he sees no sin, and even in great and egregious faults he often knows that he is not right he does not perceive the depth, the horrible enormity of the sin that is involved in them. Eye salve is one of the first medicines the Lord uses with the soul. Jesus touches the eye of the understanding, and the man becomes guilty in his own sight, as he always was guilty in the sight of God. Crimes long forgotten start up from the grave where his forgetfulness had buried them. Sins he thought were no sins suddenly rise up on their true character. And acts he thought were perfect now discover themselves to have been so mixed with evil motive that they were far from being acceptable with God. The eye is no more blind, and therefore the heart is no more proud, for the seeing eye will make a humble heart.

If I must paint a picture of penitence in this first stage, I should portray a man with his eyes bandaged walking through a path infested with the most venomous vipers, vipers that have formed a horrible girdle about his loins and are hanging like bracelets from his wrists. The man is so blind that he knows not where he is nor what it is that he fancies to be a jeweled belt upon his arm. I would then in the picture touch his eyes and bid you see his horror and astonishment when he discovers where he is and what he is. He looks behind him, and he sees through what broods of vipers he has walked. He looks before him, and he sees how thickly his future path is strewed with these venomous beasts. He looks about him, and in his living bosom looking out from his guilty heart he sees the head of a vile serpent that has twisted its coils into his very vitals. I would try, if I could, to throw into that face horror, dismay, dread, sorrow, a longing to escape, and an anxious desire to get rid of all these things that must destroy him unless he should escape from them.

And now, my dear hearers, have you ever been the subject of this divine illumination? Has God, who said to an unformed world, "Let there be light," has he said, "Let there be light" in your poor, benighted soul? Have you learned that your best deeds have been vile, and that as for your sinful acts they are ten thousand times more wicked than ever you believed them to be? I will not believe that you have ever repented unless you have first received divine illumination. I cannot expect a blind eye to see the filth upon a black hand, nor can I ever believe that the understanding that has never been enlightened can detect the sin that has stained your daily life.

Next to illumination comes humiliation. The soul having seen itself bows before God, strips itself of all its vain boasting, and lays itself flat on its face before the throne of mercy. It could talk proudly once of merit, but now it dares not pronounce the word. Once it could boast before God, with "God, I thank you that I am not as other men are," but now it stands in the distance and smites upon its breast, crying, "God be merciful to me, a sinner." Now the haughty eye, the proud look that God abhors are cast away, and the eye instead becomes a channel of tears. Its floods are perpetual, it mourns, it weeps, and the soul cries out both day and night before God, for it is vexed with itself because it has vexed the Holy Spirit and is grieved within itself because it has grieved the Most High.

Here if I had to depict penitence, I should borrow the picture of the men of Calais before our conquering king. There they kneel with ropes about their necks, clad in garments of sackcloth and ashes cast about their heads, confessing that they deserve to die. But stretching out their hands they implore mercy, and one who seems the personification of the angel of mercy—or rather, of Christ Jesus, the God of mercy—stands pleading with the king to spare their lives. Sinner, you have never repented unless that rope has been about your neck after a spiritual fashion, if you hast not felt that hell is your just desert, and that if God banish you forever from himself to the place where hope and peace can never come, he has only done with you what you have richly earned. If you have not felt that the flames of hell are the ripe harvest your sins have sown, you have never yet repented at all.

We must acknowledge the justice of the penalty as well as the guilt of the sin, or else it is but a mock repentance we pretend to possess. Down on your face, sinner, down on your face; put away you ornaments from you that he may know what to do with you. No more anoint you head and wash your face, but fast and bow your head and mourn. You have made heaven mourn, have made earth sad, and have dug hell for yourself. Confess you iniquity with shame and with confusion of face; bow down before the God of mercy and acknowledge that if he spare you it will be his free mercy that shall do it, but if he destroy you, you shall not have one word to say against the justice of the solemn sentence.

Such a stripping does the Holy Spirit give when he works this repentance, that men sometimes under it sink so low as even to long for death in order to escape from the burden that soul humiliation has cast upon them. I do not desire that you should have that terror, but I do pray that you may have no boasting left, that you may stop your mouth and feel that if now the judgment hour were set and the judgment day were come, you must stand speechless, even though God should say, "Depart, you cursed, into everlasting fire in hell." Without this I say there is no genuine evangelical repentance.

The third ingredient is detestation. The soul must go a step further than mere sorrow; it must come to hate sin, to hate the very shadow of it, to hate the house where once sin and it were boon companions, to hate the bed of pleasure and all its glittering tapestries, yea, to hate the very garments spotted with the flesh. There is no repentance where a man can talk lightly of sin, much less where he can speak tenderly and lovingly of it. When sin comes to you delicately, like Agag, saying, "Surely the bitterness of death is past," if you hast true repentance it will rise like Samuel and hew your Agag in pieces before the Lord.

As long as you harbor one idol in your heart, God will never dwell there. You must break not only the images of wood and of stone but of silver and of gold. Yea, the golden calf itself, which has been your chief idolatry, must be ground in powder and mingled in the bitter water of penitence, and you must be made to drink it. There is such a loathing of sin in the soul of the true penitent that he cannot bear its name. If you were to compel him to enter its palaces, he would be wretched. A penitent cannot bear himself in the house of the profane. He feels as if the house must fall upon him. In the assembly of the wicked he would be like a dove in the midst of ravenous kites. As well may the sheep lick blood with the wolf, as well may the dove be comrade at the vulture's feast of carrion, as a penitent sinner revel in sin. Through infirmity he may slide into it, but through grace he will rise out of it and abhor even his clothes in which he has fallen into the ditch (Job 9:31). The sinner unrepentant, like the sow, wallows in the mire. But the penitent sinner, like the swallow, may sometimes dip his wings in the limpid pool of iniquity, but he is aloft again, twittering forth with the chattering of the swallow most pitiful words of penitence, for he grieves that he should have so debased himself and sinned against his God.

My hearer, if you do not so hate your sins as to be ready to give them all up—if you are not willing now to hang them on Haman's gallows a hundred and twenty cubits high—if you cannot shake them off from you as Paul did the viper from his hand and shake it into the fire with detestation, then you know not the grace of God in truth. For if you love sin, you love neither God nor yourself, but you choose your own damnation. You are in friendship with death and in league with hell. God deliver you from this wretched state of heart and bring you to detest your sin.

There lacks one more ingredient yet. We have had illumination, humiliation, and detestation. There must be another thing, namely, a thorough transformation, for—

> Repentance is to leave
> The sins we loved before,
> And show that we in earnest grieve
> By doing so no more.

The penitent man reforms his outward life. The reform is not partial, but in heart it is universal and complete. Infirmity may mar it, but grace will always be striving against human infirmity, and the man will hate and abandon every false way. Tell me not, deceptive tradesman, that you have repented of your sin while lying placards are still upon your goods. Tell me not, you who were once a drunkard, that you have turned to God while yet the cup is dear to you and thou can still wallow in it by excess. Come not to me and say "I have repented," you avaricious wretch, while you are yet grinding your cent out of some helpless tradesman whom you have taken like a spider in your net. Come not to me and say you are forgiven when you still harbor revenge and malice against your brother and speak against your own mother's son. You lie to thine own confusion. Your face is as the whore's brazen forehead if you dare to say, "I have repented," when your arms are up to the elbow in the filth of your iniquity.

Nay, man, God will not forgive your lusts while you are still reveling in the bed of your uncleanness. And do you imagine he will forgive your drunken feasts while you are still sitting at the glutton's table! Shall he forgive your profanity when your tongue is still quivering with an oath? Think you that God shall forgive your daily transgressions when you repeat them again, and again, and again, willfully plunging into the mire? He will wash you, man, but he will not wash you for the sake of permitting you to plunge in again and defile yourself once more.

"Well," do I hear you say, "I do feel that such a change as that has taken place in me." I am glad to hear it, my dear sir, but I must ask you a further question. Divine transformation is not merely in act but in the very soul. The new man not only does not sin as he used to do, but he does not want to sin as he used to do. The pots of Egypt sometimes send up a sweet smell in his nostrils, and when he passes by another man's house, where the leek, garlic, and onion are steaming in the air, he half wishes to go back again to his Egyptian bondage. But in a moment he checks himself, saying, "No, no; the heavenly manna is better than this. The water out of the rock is sweeter than the waters of the Nile, and I cannot return to my old slavery under my old tyrant."

There may be insinuations of Satan, but his soul rejects them and agonizes to cast them out. His very heart longs to be free from every sin, and if he could be perfect, he would. There is not one sin he would spare. If you want to give him pleasure, you need not ask him to go to your haunt of debauchery; it would be the greatest pain to him you could imagine. It is not only his customs and manners but his nature that is changed. You have not put new leaves on the tree, but there is a new root to it. It is not merely new branches, but there is a new trunk altogether, and new sap, and there will be new fruit as the result of this newness. A glorious transformation is wrought by a gracious God. His penitence has become so real and so complete that the man is not the man he used to be. He is a new creature in Christ Jesus. If you are renewed by grace, and were to meet your old self, I am sure you would be very anxious to get out of his company.

"No," say you. "No, sir, I cannot accompany you."

"Why, you used to swear!"

"I cannot now."

"Well, but," says he, "you and I are very near companions."

"Yes, I know we are, and I wish we were not. You are a deal of trouble to me every day. I wish I could be rid of you forever."

"But," says Old Self, "you used to drink very well."

"Yes, I know it. I know you did, indeed, Old Self. You could sing a song as merrily as anyone. You were ringleader in all sorts of vice, but I am no relation of yours now. You are of the old Adam, and I of the new Adam. You are of your old father, the devil. But I have another—my Father who is in heaven."

I tell you, brothers, there is no man in the world you will hate so much as your old self, and there will be nothing you will so much long to get rid of as that old man who once was dragging you down to hell and who will try his hand at it over and over again every day you live and who will accomplish it yet, unless that divine grace that has made you a new man shall keep you a new man even to the end.

Good Rowland Hill, in his "Village Dialogues," gives the Christian, whom he describes in the first part of the book, the name of Thomas Newman. Ah!

And every man who goes to heaven must have the name of new man. We must not expect to enter there unless we are created anew in Christ Jesus unto good works, which God has before ordained that we should walk in them. I have thus, as best I could, feeling many and very sad distractions in my own mind, endeavored to explain the essentials of true repentance—illumination, humiliation, detestation, transformation. The endings of the words, though they are long words, may commend them to your attention and assist you to retain them.

The Companions of Repentance

Her first companion is faith. There was a question once asked by the old Puritan divines—Which was first in the soul, faith or repentance? Some said that a man could not truly repent of sin until he believed in God and had some sense of a Savior's love. Others said a man could not have faith till he had repented of sin, for he must hate sin before he could trust Christ. So a good old minister who was present remarked: "Brothers, I don't think you can ever settle this question. It would be something like asking whether, when an infant is born, the circulation of the blood or the beating of the pulse can be first observed. It seems to me that faith and repentance are simultaneous. They come at the same moment. There could be no true repentance without faith. There never was yet true faith without sincere repentance." We endorse that opinion. I believe they are like the Siamese twins; they are born together, and they could not live asunder but must die if you attempt to separate them.

Faith always walks side by side with his weeping sister, true repentance. They are born in the same house at the same hour, and they will live in the same heart every day, and on your dying bed, while you will have faith on the one hand to draw the curtain of the next world, you will have repentance, with its tears, as it lets fall the curtain upon the world from which you are departing. You will have at the last moment to weep over your own sins, and yet you shall see through that tear the place where tears are washed away. Some say there is no faith in heaven. Perhaps there is not. If there be none, then there will be no repentance, but if there be faith there will be repentance, for where faith lives, repentance must live with it. They are so united, so married and allied together, that they never can be parted, in time or in eternity. Have you, then, faith in Jesus? Does your soul look up and trust yourself in his hands? If so, then you have the repentance that needs not to be repented of.

There is another sweet thing that always goes with repentance, just as Aaron went with Moses to be spokesman for him, for you must know that Moses was slow of speech, and so is repentance. Repentance has fine eyes but stammering lips. In fact, it usually happens that repentance speaks through her eyes and cannot speak with her lips at all, except her friend—who is a good spokesman—is near. He is called Mr. Confession. This man is noted for his honesty and transparency. He knows something of himself, and he tells all that he knows before the throne of God. Confession keeps back no secrets. Repentance sighs over the sin—confession tells it out. Repentance feels the sin to be heavy within—confession plucks it forth and indicts it before the throne of God. Repentance is the soul in travail—confession delivers it. My heart is ready to burst, and there is a fire in my bones through repentance—confession gives the heavenly fire a vent, and my soul flames upward before God. Repentance alone has groanings that cannot be uttered—confession is the voice that expresses the groans. Now then, have you made confession of your sin—not to man but to God? If you have, then believe that your repentance comes from him, and it is a godly sorrow that needs not to be repented of.

Holiness is evermore the bosom friend of penitence. Fair angel, clad in pure white linen, she loves good company and will never stay in a heart where repentance is a stranger. Repentance must dig the foundations, but holiness shall erect the structure and bring forth the top stone. Repentance is the clearing away of the rubbish of the past temple of sin; holiness builds the new temple that the Lord our God shall inherit. Repentance and desires after holiness never can be separated.

Yet once more—wherever repentance is, there comes also with it peace. As Jesus walked upon the waters of Galilee and said, "Peace, be still," so peace walks over the waters of repentance and brings quiet and calm into the soul. If you would shake the thirst of your soul, repentance must be the cup out of which you drink, and then sweet peace shall be the blessed effect. Sin is such a troublesome companion that it will always give you the heartache till you have turned it out by repentance, and then your heart shall rest and be still. Sin is the rough wind that tears through the forest and sways every branch of the trees to and fro. But after penitence has come into the soul, the wind is hushed, all is still, and the birds sing in the branches of the trees that just now creaked in the storm. Sweet peace repentance ever yields to the man who possesses it. And now what do you say, my hearer—to put each point personally to you—have you had peace with God? If not, never rest till you have had it, and never believe yourself to be saved till you feel yourself to be reconciled. Be not content with the mere profession of the head, but ask that the peace of God that passes all understanding may keep your hearts and minds through Jesus Christ.

The Excellencies of Repentance

I shall somewhat surprise you, perhaps, if I say that one of the excellencies of repentance lies in its pleasantness. "Oh!" you say, "but it is bitter!" Nay, say I, it is sweet. At least, it is bitter when it is alone, like the waters of Marah, but there is a tree called the cross, which if you put into it, it will be sweet, and you will love to drink of it.

At a school of mutes who were both deaf and dumb, the teacher put the following question to her pupils: "What is the sweetest emotion?" As soon as the children comprehended the question, they took their slates and wrote their answers. One girl in a moment wrote down "joy." As soon as the teacher saw it, she expected that all would write the same, but another girl, more thoughtful, put her hand to her brow, and she wrote "hope." Verily, the girl was not far from the mark. But the next one, when she brought up her slate, had written gratitude," and this child was not wrong. Another one, when she brought up her slate, had written "love," and I am sure she was right. But there was one other who had written in large characters—and as she brought up her slate the tear was in her eye, showing she had written what she felt—"Repentance is the sweetest emotion." And I think she was right.

Verily, in my own case, after that long drought, perhaps longer than Elisha's three years in which the heavens poured forth no rain, when I saw but one tear of penitence coming from my hard, hard soul—it was such a joy! There have been times when you know you have done wrong, but when you could cry over it you have felt happy. As one weeps for his firstborn, so have you wept over your sin, and in that very weeping you have had your peace and your joy restored. I am a living witness that repentance is exceedingly sweet when mixed with divine hope, but repentance without hope is hell. It is hell to grieve for sin with the pangs of bitter remorse and yet to know that pardon can never come and mercy never be vouchsafed. Repentance, with the cross before its eyes, is heaven itself. At least, if not heaven, it is so next door to it that standing on the wet threshold I may see within the pearly portals and sing the song of the angels who rejoice within. Repentance, then, has this excellency, that it is very sweet to the soul that is made to lie beneath its shadow.

Besides this excellency, it is specially sweet to God as well as to men. "A broken and a contrite heart, O God, you will not despise." When St. Augustine lay dying, he had this verse always fixed upon the curtains, so that as often as he awoke, he might read it: "A broken and a contrite heart, O God, you will not despise." When you despise yourselves, God honors you. But as long as you honor yourselves, God despises you. A whole heart is a scentless thing, but when it is broken and bruised it is like that precious spice that was burned as holy incense in the ancient tabernacle. When the blood of Jesus is sprinkled on them, even the songs of the angels and the vials full of odors sweet that smoke before the throne of the Most High are not more agreeable to God than the sighs, groans, and tears of the brokenhearted soul. So, then, if you would be pleasing with God, come before him with many and many a tear:

> To humble souls and broken hearts
> God with his grace is ever nigh;
> Pardon and hope his love imparts,

When men in deep contrition lie.
He tells their tears, he counts their groans,
His Son redeems their souls from death;
His Spirit heals their broken bones,
They in his praise employ their breath.

John Bunyan, in his "Siege of Mansoul," when the defeated townsmen were seeking pardon, names Mr. Wet-eyes as the intercessor with the king. I hope we know Mr. Wet-eyes and have had him many times in our house, for if he cannot intercede with God, yet Mr. Wet-eyes is a great friend with the Lord Jesus Christ, and Christ will undertake his case, and then we shall prevail.

So have I set forth some, but very few, of the excellencies of repentance. And now, my dear hearers, have you repented of sin? Oh, impenitent soul, if you do not weep now, you will have to weep forever. The heart that is not broken now must be broken forever upon the wheel of divine vengeance. You must now repent, or else for ever suffer for it. Turn or burn—it is the Bible's only alternative. If you repent, the gate of mercy stands wide open. Only the Spirit of God brings you on your knees in self-abasement, for Christ's cross stands before you and he who bled upon it bids you look at him. Oh, sinner, obey the divine bidding. But, if your heart be hard, like that of the stubborn Jews in the days of Moses, take heed lest,

> The Lord in vengeance dressed,
> Shall lift his head and swear,—
> You that despised my promised rest,
> Shall have no portion there.

At any rate, sinner, if you will not repent, there is one here who will, and that is myself. I repent that I could not preach to you with more earnestness this morning and throw my whole soul more thoroughly into my pleading with you. The Lord God, whom I serve, is my constant witness that there is nothing I desire so much as to see your hearts broken on account of sin, and nothing has gladdened my heart so much as the many instances lately vouchsafed of the wonders God is doing in this place. There have been men who have stepped into this hall who had never entered a place of worship for a score years, and here the Lord has met with them. And I believe, if I could speak the word, there are hundreds who would stand up now, and say, "Twas here the Lord met with me. I was the chief of sinners; the hammer struck my heart and broke it, and now it has been bound up again by the finger of divine mercy. I tell it unto sinners, and tell it to this assembled congregation—there have been depths of mercy found that have been deeper than the depths of my iniquity."

This day there will be a soul delivered. This morning there will be, I do not doubt, despite my weakness, a display of the energy of God and the power of the Spirit. Some drunkard shall be turned from the error of his ways; some soul who was trembling on the very jaws of hell shall look to him who is the sinner's hope and find peace and pardon at this very hour. So be it, O Lord, and yours shall be the glory, world without end.

The Power of the
Risen Savior[5]

"And Jesus came and spake unto them, saying,
All power is given unto me in heaven and in
earth. Go ye therefore, and teach all nations,
baptizing them in the name of the Father,
and of the Son, and of the Holy Ghost: Teaching
them to observe all things whatsoever I have
commanded you: and, lo, I am with you always,
even unto the end of the world. Amen."
(Matthew 28:18–20)

The change from "the man of sorrows" before his crucifixion to the "Lord over all" after his

5. Published in *Metropolitan Tabernacle Pulpit*, Vol. 20 in 1874 by Charles Spurgeon. This is sermon 1200, delivered on October 25, 1874.

resurrection is striking. Before his passion he was well known by his disciples and appeared only in one form, as the Son of Man clad in the common peasant's garment without seam, woven from the top throughout. But after he had risen from the dead, he was on several occasions unrecognized by those who loved him best and is once at least described as having appeared to certain of them "under another form." He was the same person, for they saw his hands and his feet, and Thomas even handled him and placed his finger in the print of the nails. But yet it would seem that some gleams of his glory were at times manifested to them, a glory that had been hidden during his previous life, save only when he stood on the Mount of Transfiguration.

Before his death his appearances were to the general public—he stood in the midst of scribes, Pharisees, publicans, and sinners and preached the glad tidings. But now he appeared only to his disciples, sometimes to one, at another time to two, on one occasion to about five hundred brothers at once, but always to his disciples and to them only. Before his death his preaching was full of parable, plain to those who had understanding but often dark and mysterious even to his own followers, for it was a judgment from the Lord upon that evil generation that seeing they should not see and hearing they should not perceive. Yet with equal truth we may say that our Lord before his death brought down his teaching to the comprehension of the uninstructed minds that listened to it, so that many of the deeper truths were slightly touched upon because they were not able to bear them as yet.

Till his crucifixion he veiled the effulgence of many truths, but after his resurrection he spoke no more in parables but introduced his disciples into the inner circle of the great doctrines of the kingdom, and as it were showed himself face-to-face to them. Before his death the Lord Jesus was ever with his followers, and even the secret places of his retirement were known to them, but after he had risen he came and went among them at irregular intervals. Where he was during many of those forty days, who among us can tell? He was seen in the garden upon Olivet, he walked to Emmaus, he comforted the assembly at Jerusalem, he showed himself again to the disciples at the Sea of Tiberias, but where went he when, after the various interviews, he vanished out of their sight? They were in the room alone, the doors were shut, and suddenly he stood in the midst of them. Again he called to them from the beach, and on landing they found a fire of coals kindled and fish laid thereon and bread. His appearances were strange and his disappearances equally so. Everything betokened that, after he had risen from the dead, he had undergone some marvelous change that had revealed in him what had been concealed before, though still his identity was indisputable.

It was no small honor to have seen our risen Lord while he lingered here below. What must it be to see Jesus as he is now! He is the same Jesus as when he was here; yonder memorials as of a lamb that has been slain assure us that he is the same man. Glorified in heaven his real manhood sits, and it is capable of being beheld by the eye and heard by the ear, but yet how different. Had we seen him in his agony, we should all the more admire his glory. Dwell with your hearts very much upon Christ crucified, but indulge yourselves often with a sight of Christ glorified. Delight to think that he is not here, for he is risen. He is not here, for he has ascended. He is not here, for he sits at the right hand of God and makes intercession for us. Let your souls travel frequently the blessed highway from the sepulcher to the throne. As in Rome there was a Via Sacra along which returning conquerors went from the gates of the city up to the heights of the capitol, so is there another Via Sacra that you ought often to survey, for along it the risen Savior went in glorious majesty from the tomb of Joseph of Arimathea up to the eternal dignities of his Father's right hand. Your soul will do well to see her dawn of hope in his death and her full assurance of hope in his risen life.

Today my business is to show, as far as God the Spirit may help me, first, our Lord's resurrection power, and secondly, our Lord's mode of exercising the spiritual part of that power so far as we are concerned.

Jesus's Resurrection Power

"All power is given unto me in heaven and in earth." At the risk of repeating myself, I should like to begin this head by asking you to remember last Sabbath morning's sermon, when we went to Gethsemane and bowed our spirits in the shade of those grey olives at the sight of the bloody sweat. What a contrast between that and this! There you saw the weakness of man, the bowing, the prostrating, the crushing of the manhood of the Mediator, but here you see the strength of the God-Man: he is girt with omnipotence, though still on earth when he spoke these words he had received a privilege, honor, glory, fullness, and power that lifted him far above the sons of men. He was, as Mediator, no more a sufferer but a sovereign, no more a victim but a victor, no more a servant but the monarch of earth and heaven. Yet he had never received such power if he had not endured such weakness. All power had never been given to the Mediator if all comfort had not been taken away. He stooped to conquer. The way to his throne was downward. Mounting upon steps of ivory, Solomon ascended to his throne of gold. But our Lord and Master descended that he might ascend and went down into the awful deeps of agony unutterable that all power in heaven and earth might belong to him as our Redeemer and Covenant Head.

Now think a moment of these words, "All power." Jesus Christ has given to him by his Father, as a consequence of his death, "all power." It is but another way of saying that the Mediator possesses omnipotence, for omnipotence is but the Latin of "all power." What mind shall conceive, what tongue shall set in order before you the meaning of all power? We cannot grasp it. It is high, we cannot attain unto it. Such knowledge is too wonderful for us. The power of self-existence, the power of creation, the power of sustaining that which is made, the power of fashioning and destroying, the power of opening and shutting, of overthrowing or establishing, of killing and making alive, the power to pardon and to condemn, to give and to withhold, to decree and to fulfill, to be, in a word, "head over all things to his church"—all this is vested in Jesus Christ our Lord. We might as well attempt to describe infinity or map the boundless as to tell what "all power" must mean. But whatever it is, it is all given to our Lord, all lodged in those hands that once were fastened to the wood of shame, all left with that heart that was pierced with the spear, all placed as a crown upon that head that was surrounded with a coronet of thorns.

"All power in heaven" is his. Observe that! Then he has the power of God, for God is in heaven, and the power of God emanates from that central throne. Jesus, then, has divine power. Whatever Yahweh can do, Jesus can do. If it were his will to speak another world into existence, we should see tonight a fresh star adorning the brow of night. Were it his will at once to fold up creation like a worn-out vesture, lo the elements would pass away and yonder heavens would be shriveled like a scroll. The power that binds the sweet influences of the Pleiades and looses the bands of Orion is with the Nazarene. The Crucified leads forth Arcturus with his sons. Angelic bands are waiting on the wing to do the bidding of Jesus of Nazareth, and cherubim and seraphim and the four living creatures before the throne unceasingly obey him. He who was despised and rejected of men now commands the homage of all heaven, as "God over all, blessed forever."

"All power in heaven" relates to the providential skill and might with which God rules everything in the universe. He holds the reins of all created forces and impels or restrains them at his will, giving force to law and life to all existence. The old heathen dreamed of Apollo as driving the chariot of the sun and guiding its fiery steeds in their daily course, but it is not so: Jesus is Lord of all. He harnesses the winds to his chariot and thrusts a bit into the mouth of the tempest, doing as he wills among the armies of heaven and the inhabitants of this lower world. From him in heaven emanates the power that sustains and governs this globe, for the Father has committed all things into his hands: "By him all things consist."

"All power" must include—and this is a practical point to us—all the power of the Holy Spirit. In the work that lies nearest our heart the Holy Spirit is the great force. It is he who convinces men of sin, leads them to a Savior, gives them new hearts and right spirits, plants them in the church, and then causes them to grow and become fruitful. The power of the Holy Spirit goes forth among the sons of men according to the will of our Lord. As the anointing oil poured upon Aaron's head ran down his beard and bedewed the skirts of his garments, so the Spirit that has been granted to him without measure flows from him to us. He has the residue of the Spirit, and according to his will the Holy Spirit goes forth into the church, and from the church into the world, to the accomplishment of the purposes of saving grace. It is not possible that the church should fail for want of spiritual gifts or influence while her heavenly Bridegroom has such overflowing stores of both.

All the power of the sacred Trinity—Father, Son, and Spirit—is at the command of Jesus, who is exalted far above all principality, power, might, dominion, and every name that is named, not only in this world but in that which is to come.

Our Lord also claimed that all power had been given to him on earth. This is more than could be truly said by any mere man; none of mortal race may claim all power in heaven, and when they aspire to all power on earth it is but a dream. Universal monarchy has been strained after; it has seldom, if ever, been attained. And when it seemed within the clutch of ambition, it has melted away like a snowflake before the sun. Indeed, if men could rule all their fellows, yet they would not have all power on earth, for there are other forces that scorn their control. Fell diseases laugh at the power of men. The king of Israel, when

Naaman came to him to be recovered of his leprosy, cried, "Am I God, to kill and to make alive, that this man does send unto me to recover a man of his leprosy?" He had not all power.

Winds and waves, moreover, scorn mortal rule. It is not true that even Britannia rules the waves. Canute, to rebuke his courtiers, places his throne at the margin of the tide and commands the billows to take care that they wet not the feet of their royal master, but his courtiers were soon covered with spray and the monarch proved that "all power" was not given to him.

Frogs and locusts and flies were more than a match for Pharaoh; the greatest of men are defeated by the weak things of God. Nebuchadnezzar, struck with madness and herding with cattle, was an illustration of the shadowy nature of all human power. The proudest princes have been made to feel by sickness, pain, and death that after all they were but men, and oftentimes their weaknesses have been such as to make the more apparent the truth that power belongs to God and God alone, so that when he entrusts a little of it to the sons of men, it is so little that they are fools if they boast thereof. See, then, before us a wonder. A man who has power over all things on earth without exception and is obeyed by all creatures great and small, because the Lord Yahweh has put all things under his feet.

For our purposes it will be most important to remember that our Lord has "all power" over the minds of men, both good and bad. He calls whoever he pleases into his fellowship, and they obey. Having called them, he is able to sanctify them to the highest point of holiness, working in them all the good pleasure of his will with power. The saints can be so influenced by our Lord, through the Holy Spirit, that they can be impelled to the divinest ardors and elevated to the sublimest frames of mind.

Often do I pray, and I doubt not the prayer has come from you too, that God would raise up leaders in the church, men full of faith and of the Holy Spirit, standard-bearers in the day of battle. The preachers of the gospel who preach with any power are few; still might Paul say, "You have not many fathers." More precious than the gold of Ophir are men who stand out as pillars of the Lord's house, bulwarks of the truth, champions in the camp of Israel. How few are our apostolic men! We want again Luthers, Calvins, Bunyans, Whitfields, men fit to mark eras whose names breathe terror in our foemen's ears. We have dire need of such. Where are they? Whence will they come to us? We cannot tell in what farmhouse, village smithy, or schoolhouse such men may be, but our Lord has them in store. They are the gifts of Jesus Christ to the church and will come in due time. He has power to give us back again a golden age of preachers, a time as fertile of great divines and mighty ministers as the Puritan age, which many of us account to have been the golden age of theology. He can send again the men of studious heart to search the Word and bring forth its treasures, the men of wisdom and experience rightly to divide it, the golden-mouthed speakers who, either as sons of thunder or sons of consolation, shall deliver the message of the Lord with the Holy Spirit sent down from heaven. When the Redeemer ascended on high he received gifts for men, and those gifts were men fitted to accomplish the edification of the church, such as evangelists, pastors, and teachers. These he is still able to bestow upon his people, and it is their duty to pray for them, and when they come to receive them with gratitude. Let us believe in the power of Jesus to give us valiant men and men of renown, and we little know how soon he will supply them.

Since all power on earth is lodged in Christ's hands, he can also clothe any and all of his servants with a sacred might by which their hands shall be sufficient for them in their high calling. Without bringing them forth into the front ranks, he can make them occupy their appointed stations till he comes, girt with a power that shall make them useful. My brother, the Lord Jesus can make you eminently prosperous in the sphere in which he has placed you; my sister, your Lord can bless the little children who gather at your knee through your means. You are very feeble, and you know it, but there is no reason why you should not be strong in him. If you look to the strong for strength, he can endue you with power from on high and say to you as to Gideon, "Go in this your might." Your slowness of speech need not disqualify you, for he will be with your mouth as with Moses. Your want of culture need not hinder you, for Shamgar with his ox goad smote the Philistines, and Amos the prophet was a herdsman. Like Paul, your personal presence may be despised as weak, and your speech as contemptible, but yet like him you may learn to glory in infirmity because the power of God does rest upon you. You are not impoverished in the Lord but in yourselves, if impoverished at all.

You may be as dry as Aaron's rod, but he can make you bud and blossom and bring forth fruit. You may be as nearly empty as the widow's jar, yet will he cause you still to overflow towards his saints. You may feel yourself to be as near sinking as Peter amid the waves, yet will he keep you from your fears. You may be as unsuccessful as the disciples who had toiled all night and taken nothing, yet he can fill your boat till it can hold no more. No man knows what the Lord can make of him, nor what he may do by him, only this we do know assuredly: that "all power" is with him by whom we were redeemed, and to whom we belong.

Oh, believers, resort to your Lord to receive out of his fullness grace for grace. Because of this power we believe that if Jesus willed, he could stir the whole church at once to the utmost energy. Does she sleep? His voice can awaken her. Does she restrain prayer? His grace can stimulate her to devotion. Has she grown unbelieving? He can restore her ancient faith. Does she turn her back in the day of battle, troubled with skepticism and doubts? He can restore her unwavering confidence in the gospel and make her valiant till all her sons shall be heroes of faith and put to flight the armies of the aliens.

Let us believe, and we shall see the glory of God. Let us believe, I say, and once again our conquering days shall come, when one shall chase a thousand and two shall put ten thousand to flight. Never despair for the church; be anxious for her and turn your anxiety into prayer, but be hopeful evermore, for her Redeemer is mighty and will stir up his strength. "The

Lᴏʀᴅ of Hosts is with us; the God of Jacob is our refuge." Degenerate as we are, there stands one among us whom the world sees not, whose shoe's latchet we are not worthy to unloose. He shall again baptize us with the Holy Spirit and with fire, for "all power is given unto him."

It is equally true that all power is given unto our Lord over the whole of mankind, even over that part of the race that rejects and continues in willful rebellion. He can use the ungodly for his purposes. We have it on inspired authority that Herod and Pilate, with the Gentiles and the people of Israel, were gathered together to do whatsoever the Lord's hand and counsel determined before to be done. Their utmost wickedness did but fullfil the determinate counsel of God. Thus does he make wrath of man to praise him and the most rebellious wills to be subservient to his sacred purposes.

Jesus's kingdom rules over all. The powers of hell and all their hosts, with the kings of the earth and the rulers set themselves and take counsel together, and all the while their rage is working out his designs. Little do they know that they are but drudges to the King of kings, scullions in the kitchen of his imperial palace. All things do his bidding. His will is not thwarted. His resolves are not defeated. The pleasure of the Lord prospers in his hands. By faith I see him ruling and overruling on land and sea and in all deep places. Guiding the decisions of parliaments, dictating to dictators, commanding princes, and ruling emperors. Let him but arise, and they that hate him shall flee before him; as smoke is driven, so will he drive them away; as wax melts before the fire, so shall all his enemies perish at his presence.

As to sinful men in general, the Redeemer has power over their minds in a manner wonderful to contemplate. At the present moment we very much deplore the fact that the current of public thought runs strongly towards Popery, which is the alias of idolatry. Just as in Old Testament history the people of Israel were always breaking away after their idols, so is it with this nation. The Israelites were cured of their sin for a little while, so long as some great teacher or judge had power among them, but at his death they turned aside to worship the queen of heaven, the calves of Bethel, or some other visible symbols. So it is now. Men are mad after the idols of old Rome. They are turning the old churches into Chinese temples and building new ones on all sides. Idol temples are becoming as numerous in London as in Calcutta. The worshipers and priests call themselves Christians, but they might better call themselves wafer-worshipers or adorers of a fetish made of flour and water, for that is nearer the truth.

Well, what next? Are we despairing? God forbid that we should ever despond while all power is in the hand of Jesus. He can turn the whole current of thought in an opposite direction, and that right speedily. Did you not observe when the Prince of Wales was ill some months ago that everybody paid respect to the doctrine of prayer? Did you not notice how the *Times* and other newspapers spoke right believingly as to prayer? At this moment it is fashionable to poohpooh the idea of God's hearing our requests, but it was not so then. A great philosopher has told us that it is absurd to suppose that prayer can have any effect upon the events of life, but God has only to visit the nation with some judgment severely felt by all and your philosopher will become as quiet as a mouse.

In the same way, I am firmly persuaded that, by one turn of the wheel of Providence, the Popery that is now so fashionable will be made, as it has been before, a red rag to set mobs a rioting, and my lords and ladies, instead of hastening to the Pope, will be most anxious to disown all connection with the whole concern. To my mind it matters very little which way these fine folks go at any time, except that they are the straws that show which way the wind blows. I repeat it, the current of thought can readily be turned by our Lord; he can as easily manage it as the miller controls the stream that flows over his wheel or rushes past it. The times are safe in our Redeemer's management. He is mightier than the devil, the Pope, the infidel, and the ritualist all put together. All glory be to him who has all power in earth and heaven.

So too, our Lord can give, and he does give to the people an inclination to hear the gospel. Never be afraid of getting a congregation when the gospel is your theme. Jesus, who gives you a consecrated tongue, will find willing ears to listen to you. At his bidding deserted sanctuaries grow crowded, and the people throng to hear the joyful sound. Ay, and he can do more than that, for he can make the word powerful to the conversion of thousands. He can constrain the frivolous to think, the obstinately heretical to accept the truth, and those who set their faces like flint to yield to his gracious sway. He has the key to every human heart. He opens, and no man shuts: he shuts, and no man opens. He will clothe his word with power and subdue the nations thereby.

It is ours to proclaim the gospel and to believe that no man is beyond the saving power of Jesus Christ. Doubly dyed, yea, sevenfold steeped in the scarlet dye of vice, the sinner may be cleansed, and the ringleader in vice may become a pattern of holiness. The Pharisee can be converted—was not Paul? Even priests may be saved, for did not a great multitude of the priests believe? There is no man in any conceivable position of sin who is beyond the power of Christ. He may be gone to the uttermost in sin, so as to stand on the verge of hell, but if Jesus stretches out his pierced hand, he will be plucked like a brand out of the burning.

My soul glows as I think of what my Lord can do. If all power is given unto him in heaven and in earth, then this morning he could convert, pardon, and save every man and woman in this place. Nay, he could influence the four millions of this city to cry, "What must we do to be saved?" Nor in this city only could he work, but throughout the whole earth. If it seemed good to his infinite wisdom and power he could make every sermon the means of conversion of all who heard it, every Bible and every copy of the Word the channel of salvation to all who read it, and I know not in how short a time the cry would be heard, "Hallelujah, for the Lord God omnipotent reigns." Heard that cry shall be, rest assured of that. We are on the conquering side. We have with us One who is infinitely greater than all that can be against us, since "all power" is given unto him.

Brothers, we have no doubts and entertain no fears, for every moment of time is bringing on the grand display of the power of Jesus. We preach today, and some of you despise the gospel; we bring Christ before you, and you reject him. But God will change his hand with you before long, and your despisings and your rejectings will then come to an end, for that same Jesus who went from Olivet and ascended into heaven will so come in like manner as he was seen to go up into heaven. He will descend with matchless pomp and power, and this astonished world that saw him crucified shall see him enthroned. In the selfsame place where men dogged his heels and persecuted him, they shall crowd around him to pay him homage, for he must reig, and put his enemies under his feet. This same earth shall be gladdened by his triumphs that once was troubled with his griefs. And more.

You may be dead before the Lord shall come, and your bodies may be rotting in the tomb, but you will know that all power is his, for at the blast of his trumpet your bodies shall rise again to stand before his terrible judgment seat. You may have resisted him here, but you will be unable to oppose him then. You may despise him now, but then you must tremble before him. "Depart, you cursed" will be to you a terrible proof that he has "all power" if you will not now accept another and a sweeter proof of it by coming unto him who bids the laboring and heavy laden partake of his rest. "Kiss the Son, lest he be angry, and you perish from the way, when his wrath is kindled but a little. Blessed are all they that put their trust in him."

How Jesus Exercises His Great Power

I have, secondly, by your patience, to show our Lord's usual mode of exercising his great spiritual power. Brothers, the Lord Jesus might have said, "All power is given to me in heaven and earth; take then your swords and slay all these my enemies who crucified me." But he had no thoughts of revenge. He might have said, "These Jews put me to death; therefore, go straightway to the Isles and to Tarshish and preach, for these men shall never taste of my grace." But no, he expressly said "beginning at Jerusalem" and bade his disciples first preach the gospel to his murderers.

In consequence of his having "all power," his servants were bidden to disciple all nations. My brothers, the method by which Jesus proposes to subdue all things unto himself appears to be utterly inadequate. To teach, to make disciples, to baptize these disciples, and to instruct them further in the faith! Good Master, are these the weapons of our warfare? Are these your battle-ax and weapons of war? Not thus do the princes of this world contemplate conquest, for they rely on monster guns, ironclads, and engines of death-doing power. Yet what are these but proofs of their weakness? Had they all power in themselves, they would not need such instruments. Only he who has all power can work his bidding by a word and dispense with all force but that of love.

Mark that teaching and preaching are the Lord's way of displaying his power. Today they tell us that the way to save souls is to rig out an altar with different colored silks and satins, variable according to the almanac, and to array priests in garments of divers colors—"of divers colors of needlework, on both sides, meet for the necks of them that take the spoil"—and to make men wear petticoats, dishonorable to their sex. With these ribbons and embroideries, joined with incense burning, posturing, and incantations, souls are to be saved! "Not so," says the Master, but "Go into all the world, and preach the gospel to every creature."

Do any of you fear that, after all, the preaching of the gospel will be defeated in this land of ours by these new editions of the old idolatry? God forbid. If there were only one of us left to preach the gospel, he would be a match for ten thousand priests. Only give us still the tongue set on fire by the Holy Spirit and an open Bible, and one solitary preacher would rout the whole rabble of your monks and friars and father-confessors, sisters of misery, nuns, pilgrims, bishops, cardinals, and popes, because preaching and teaching and baptizing the disciples are Christ's way. Priestcraft is not Christ's way. If Christ had ordained sacramental efficacy, it would succeed, but he has ordained nothing of the kind. His mandate is: "All power is given unto me in heaven and earth, go, therefore, disciple, baptize, and then still further instruct in the name of the Triune God."

My brothers, remember who the men were who were sent on this errand. The eleven who were foremost were mostly fishermen. Does the omnipotent Jesus choose fishermen to subdue the world? He does, because he needs no help from them; all power is his. We must have an educated ministry, they tell us; and by "an educated ministry" they mean, not the ministry of a man of common sense, clear head and warm heart, deep experience, and large acquaintance with human nature, but the ministry of mere classical and mathematical students, theorists, and novices, more learned in modern infidelities than in the truth of God.

Our Lord, if he had wished to employ the worldly wise, might certainly have chosen an eleven in Corinth or in Athens who would have commanded general respect for their attainments, or he could have found eleven learned rabbis near at home. But he did not want such men; their vaunted attainments were of no value in his eyes. He chose honest, hearty men who were childlike enough to learn the truth and bold enough to speak it when they knew it. The church must get rid of her notion that she must depend on the learning of this world. Against a sound education we cannot have a word to say, especially an education in the Scriptures, but to place learned degrees in the place of the gift of the Holy Spirit or to value the present style of so-called culture above the spiritual edification of our manhood is to set up an idol in the house of the living God. The Lord can as well use the most illiterate man as the most learned, if so it pleases him. "Go," he said, "fishermen, go, and teach all to nations." Carnal reason's criticism on this is a feeble method to be worked out by feebler instruments!

Now let it be noted here that the work of preaching the gospel, which is Christ's way of using his power among men, is based only upon his having that power. Hearken to some of my brothers; they say, "You must not preach the gospel to a dead sinner,

THE POWER OF THE RISEN SAVIOR

because the sinner has no power." Just so, but our reason for preaching to him is that all power is given unto Jesus, and he bids us preach the gospel to every creature. "But when you tell a sinner to believe, you have not the power to make him believe." Truly so, nor do we dream that we have, for all power lies in Christ. Neither in the sinner is there power to believe, nor in the preacher power to make him believe; all power is in our Lord. "But do you think," say they, "that your persuasions will ever make a man repent and believe?" Certainly not. The power that leads men to repent and believe does not lie in rhetoric, in reason, or in persuasion, but in him who says, "All power is given unto me in heaven and in earth."

I tell you this, if my Lord and Master should bid me go tomorrow to Norwood Cemetery and bid the dead to rise, I would do it with as much pleasure as I now preach the gospel to this congregation. And I would do it for the same reason that now leads me to urge the unregenerated to repent and be converted, for I regard men as being dead in sin, and yet I tell them to live, because my Master commands me do so. That I am right in thus acting is proved by the fact that while I am preaching, sinners do live. Blessed be his name, thousands of them have been quickened into life.

Ezekiel had to cry, "Dry bones, live." What a foolish thing to say! But God justified his servant in it, and an exceeding great army stood upon their feet in what was once a large charnel house. Joshua's men were bidden to blow their trumpets around Jericho—a most absurd thing to blow a trumpet to fetch city walls down—but they came down for all that. Gideon's men were bidden simply to carry lamps within their pitchers, to break their pitchers, and stand still and cry aloud, "The sword of the Lord and of Gideon"—a most ridiculous thing to hope by this means to smite the Midianites—but they were smitten, for God never sends his servants on a fool's errand.

It pleases God by the foolishness of preaching to accomplish his divine purposes, not because of the power of preaching, nor the power of the preacher, nor any power in those preached to, but because "all power" is given unto Christ "in heaven and in earth," and he chooses to work by the teaching of the Word.

Our business, then, is just this. We are to teach, or as the Greek word has it, to make disciples. Our business is, each one according to the grace given, to tell our fellow men the gospel and to try and disciple them to Jesus. When they become disciples, our next duty is to give them the sign of discipleship by "baptizing them." That symbolic burial sets forth their death in

Jesus to their former selves and their resurrection to newness of life through him.

Baptism enrolls and seals the disciples, and we must not omit or misplace it. When the disciple is enrolled, the missionary is to become the pastor, "teaching them to observe all things whatsoever I have commanded you." The disciple is admitted into the school by obeying the Savior's command as to baptism, and then he goes on to learn, and as he learns he teaches others also. He is taught obedience, not to some things but to all things Christ has commanded. He is put into the church not to become a legislator or a deviser of new doctrines and ceremonies but to believe what Christ tells him and to do what Christ bids him.

Thus our Lord intends to set up a kingdom that shall break in pieces every other. Those who know him are to teach others, and so from one to the other the wondrous power that Christ brought from heaven shall spread from land to land. See, then, my brothers, your high calling, and see also the support you have in pursuing it. In the van behold "all power" going forth from Christ! In the rear behold the Lord himself, "Lo, I am with you always, even unto the end of the world." If you are enlisted in this army, I charge you be faithful to your great captain. Do his work carefully in the way he has prescribed for you and expect to see his power displayed to his own glory.

I would close this sermon very practically. The greater part of my congregation at this time consists of persons who have believed in Jesus, who have been baptized, and who have been further instructed. You believe that Jesus has all power and that he works through the teaching and preaching of the gospel, and therefore I wish to press you with a home question. How much are you doing as to teaching all nations? This charge is committed to you as well as to me. For this purpose are we sent into the world, ourselves receivers that we may be afterwards distributors. How much have you distributed? Dear brother, dear sister, to how many have you told the story of redemption by the blood of Jesus? You have been a convert now for some time; to whom have you spoken of Jesus, or to whom have you written? Are you distributing as best you can the words of others if you are not capable of putting words together yourself?

Do not reply, "I belong to a church which is doing much." That is not to the point. I am speaking of that which you are personally doing. Jesus did not die for us by proxy, but he bore our sins in his own body on the tree. I ask, then, what are you personally doing? Are you doing anything at all? "But I cannot go for a missionary," says one. Are you sure you cannot? I have been long looking for a time when numbers of you will feel that you must go to preach the gospel abroad and will relinquish comforts and emoluments for the Lord's sake. I shall never feel that we have reached the full degree of Christian zeal until it becomes a very common thing among us to have young brothers, such as the two who left us a little while ago, consecrating themselves to the grandest of all services. Perhaps some among you have that intent half-formed in your hearts; I hope you will not repress it and that your parents will not hinder you from the blessed sacrifice. There can be no greater honor to a church than to have many sons and daughters bearing the brunt of the battle for the Lord.

Lo, I set up a standard among you this day. Let those whose hearts God has touched rally to it without delay. The heathen are perishing; they are dying by millions without Christ, and Christ's last command to us is "Go, teach all nations." Are you obeying it? "I cannot go," says one, "I have a family and many ties to bind me at home." My dear brother, then, I ask you, are you going as far as you can? Do you travel to the utmost length of the providential tether that has fastened you where you are? Can you say "Yes"? Then, what are you doing to help others to go?

As I was thinking over this discourse, I reflected how very little we were most of us doing towards sending the gospel abroad. We are, as a church, doing a fair share for our heathen at home, and I rejoice at the thought of i. But how much a year do you each give to foreign missions? I wish you would put down in your pocketbook how much you give per annum for missions and then calculate how much percent it is of your income. There let it stand—"Item: Gave to the collection last April ... Is." One shilling a year towards the salvation of the world. Perhaps it will run thus—"Item: Income £5000, annual subscription to mission £1." How does that look? I cannot read your hearts, but I could read your pocketbooks and work a sum in proportion. I suggest that you do it yourselves while I also take a look at my own expenditure. Let us all see what more can be done for the spread of the Redeemer's kingdom, for all power is with him. And when his people shall be stirred up to believe in that power and to use the simple but potent machinery of the preaching of the gospel to all nations, then God, even our own God, shall bless us, and all the ends of the earth shall fear him. Amen.

Soul Winning[6]

"He that winneth souls is wise."
(Proverbs 11:30)

The text does not say, "he that wins sovereigns is wise," though no doubt he thinks himself wise, and perhaps, in a certain groveling sense in these days of competition, he must be so. But such wisdom is of the earth and ends with the earth, and there is another world where the currencies of Europe will not be accepted, nor their past possession be any sign of wealth or wisdom.

6. Published in *Metropolitan Tabernacle Pulpit*, Vol. 15 in 1869 by Charles Spurgeon. This is sermon 850, delivered in 1869, exact date unknown.

Solomon, in the text before us, awards no crown for wisdom to crafty statesmen or even to the ablest of rulers; he issues no diplomas even to philosophers, poets, or men of wit; he crowns with laurel only those who win souls. He does not declare that he who preaches is necessarily wise—and alas! there are multitudes who preach and gain much applause and eminence, who win no souls and who shall find it go hard with them at the last, because in all probability they have run and the Master has never sent them.

He does not say that he who talks about winning souls is wise, since to lay down rules for others is a very simple thing, but to carry them out oneself is far more difficult. He who actually, really, and truly trims men from the error of their ways to God, and so is made the means of saving them from going down to hell, is a wise man. And that is true of him whatever his style of soul winning may be. He may be a Paul, deeply logical, profound in doctrine, able to command all candid judgments; and if he thus wins souls he is wise. He may be an Apollos, grandly rhetorical, whose lofty genius soars into the very heaven of eloquence; and if he wins souls in that way he is wise, but not otherwise. Or he may be a Cephas, rough and rugged, using uncouth metaphor and stern declamation, but if he wins souls he is no less wise than his polished brother or his argumentative friend, but not else.

The great wisdom of soul winners, according to the text, is proven only by their actual success in really winning souls. To their own Master they are accountable for how they go to work, not to us. Do not let us be comparing and contrasting this minister and that. Who are you who judges another man's servants? Wisdom is justified in all her children. Only children wrangle about incidental methods; men look at sublime results. Do these workers of many sorts and divers manners win souls? Then they are wise; and you who criticize them, being yourselves unfruitful, cannot be wise, even though you affect to be their judges. God proclaims soul winners to be wise, dispute it who dare. This degree from the College of Heaven may surely stand them in good stead, let their fellow mortals say what they will of them.

"He that wins souls is wise," and this can be seen very clearly. He must be a wise man in even ordinary respects who can by grace achieve so divine a marvel. Great soul winners never have been fools. A man whom God qualifies to win souls could probably do anything else that providence might allot him. Take Martin Luther. Why, sirs, the man was not only fit to work a Reformation, but he could have ruled a nation or commanded an army. Think of Whitfield, and remember that the thundering eloquence that stirred all England was not associated with a weak judgment or an absence of brain power; the man was a master orator, and if he had addicted himself to commerce, he would have taken a chief place among the merchants. Or had he been a politician, amid admiring senates would have commanded the listening ear. He that wins souls is usually a man who could have done anything else if God had called him to it.

I know the Lord uses what means he wills, but he always uses means suitable to the end. And if you tell me that David slew Goliath with a sling, I answer—it was the best weapon in the world to reach so tall a giant, and the very fittest weapon that David could have used, for he had been skilled in it from his youth up. There is always an adaptation in the instruments that God uses to produce the ordained result, and though the glory is not to them, nor the excellence in them, but all is to be ascribed to God, yet is there a fitness and preparedness that God sees, even if we do not. It is assuredly true that soul winners are by no means idiots or simpletons, but such as God makes wise for himself, though vainglorious wiseacres may dub them fools.

"He that wins souls is wise," because he has selected a wise object. I think it was Michelangelo who once carved certain magnificent statues in snow. They are gone; the material readily compacted by the frost as readily melted in the heat. Far wiser was he when he fashioned the enduring marble and produced works that will last all down the ages. But even marble itself is consumed and fretted by the tooth of time, and he is wise who selects for his raw material immortal souls, whose existence shall outlast the stars. If God shall bless us to the winning of souls, our work shall remain when the wood, hay, and stubble of earth's art and science shall have gone to the dust from which they sprang.

In heaven itself the soul winner, blessed of God, shall have memorials of his work preserved for ever in the galleries of the skies. He has selected a wise object, for what can be wiser than to glorify God, and what, next to that, can be wiser than in the highest sense to bless our fellow men, to snatch a soul from the gulf that yawns, to lift it up to the heaven that glorifies, to deliver an immortal from the bondage of Satan, and to bring him into the liberty of Christ? What more excellent than this? I say that such an aim would commend itself to all right minds, and that angels themselves may envy us poor sons of men that we are permitted to make this our life object, to win souls for Jesus Christ. Wisdom herself assents to the excellence of the design.

To accomplish such a work, a man must be wise, for to win a soul requires infinite wisdom. God himself wins not souls without wisdom, for the eternal plan of salvation was dictated by an infallible judgment, and in every line of it infinite skill is apparent. Christ, God's great soul winner, is "the wisdom of God" as well as "the power of God." There is as much wisdom to be seen in the new creation as in the old. In a sinner saved, there is as much of God to be beheld as in a universe rising out of nothing. And we, then, who are to be workers together with God, proceeding side by side with him to the great work of soul winning, must be wise too. It is a work that filled a Savior's heart—a work that moved the eternal mind or ever the earth was. It is no child's play, nor a thing to be achieved while we are half asleep, nor to be attempted without deep consideration, nor to be carried on without gracious help from the only wise God, our Savior. The pursuit is wise.

Mark well, my brothers, that he who is successful in soul winning will prove to have been a wise man in the judgment of those who see the end as well as the beginning. Even if I were utterly selfish and had no care for anything but my own happiness, I would choose, if I might, under God, to be a soul winner, for never did I know perfect, overflowing, unutterable happiness of the purest and most ennobling order till I first heard of one who had sought and found a Savior through my means. I recollect the thrill of joy that went through me! No young mother ever rejoiced so much over her first-born child; no warrior was so exultant over a hard-won victory. Oh! the joy of knowing that a sinner once at enmity has been reconciled to God, by the Holy Spirit, through the words spoken by our feeble lips. Since then, by grace given to me, the thought of which prostrates me in self-abasement, I have seen and heard of not hundreds only, but even thousands of sinners turned from the error of their ways by the testimony of God in me.

Let afflictions come, let trials be multiplied as God wills, still this joy preponderates above all others, the joy that we are unto God a sweet savor of Christ in every place and that as often as we preach the Word, hearts are unlocked, bosoms heave with a new life, eyes weep for sin, and their tears are wiped away as they see the great Substitute for sin and live. Beyond all controversy, it is a joy worth worlds to win souls, and—thank God—it is a joy that does not cease with this mortal life. It must be no small bliss to hear, as one wings his flight up to the eternal throne, the wings of others fluttering at one's side towards the same glory, and turning round and questioning them, to hear them say, "We are entering with you through the gates of pearl. You brought us to the Savior." To be welcomed to the skies by those who call us father in God, father in better bonds than those of earth, father through grace and sire for immortality—it will be bliss beyond compare to meet in you eternal seats with those begotten of us in Christ Jesus, for whom we travailed in birth till Christ was formed in them the hope of glory. This is to have many heavens, a heaven in every one won for Christ, according to the Master's promise "they that turn many to righteousness, shall shine as the stars for ever and ever."

I have said enough, brothers, I trust, to make some of you desire to occupy the position of soul winners, but before I further address myself to my text, I should like to remind you that the honor does not belong to ministers only. They may take their full share of it, but it belongs to every one of you who have devoted yourselves to Christ; such honor have all the saints. Every man here, every woman here, and every child here whose heart is right with God may be a soul-winner. There is no man placed by God's providence where he cannot do good. There is not a glowworm under a hedge but gives a needed light, and there is not a laboring man, a suffering woman, a servant girl, a chimney sweeper, or a crossing sweeper but what has opportunities for serving God. And what I have said of soul winners belongs not to the learned doctor of divinity or to the eloquent preacher alone but to you all who are in Christ Jesus. You can, each of you, if grace enable you, be thus wise and win the happiness of turning souls to Christ through the Holy Spirit.

I am about to dwell upon my text in this way: "He that wins souls is wise." I shall, first, make that fact stand out a little clearer by explaining the metaphor used in the text—winning souls. And then, secondly, by giving you some lessons in the matter of soul winning, through which I trust the conviction will be forced upon each believing mind that the work needs the highest wisdom.

The Metaphor Used in the Text

We use the word "win" in many ways. It is sometimes found in very bad company, in those games of chance, juggling tricks, sleight-of-hand, or thimble-rigging (to use a plain word), which sharpers are so fond of winning by. I am sorry to say that much of legerdemain and trickery are to be met with in the religious world. Why, there are those who pretend to save souls by curious tricks, intricate maneuvers, and dexterous posture making. A basin of water, half a dozen drops, certain syllables—heigh, presto!—the infant is a child of grace and becomes a member of Christ and an inheritor of the kingdom of heaven. This aqueous regeneration surpasses my belief; it is a trick I do not understand. The initiated only can perform the beautiful piece of magic, which excels anything ever attempted by the Wizard of the North.

There is a way, too, of winning souls by laying hands upon heads, only the elbows of aforesaid hands must be encased in lawn, and then the machinery acts, and there is grace conferred by blessed fingers! I must confess I do not understand the occult science, but at this I need not wonder, for the profession of saving souls by such juggling can only be carried out by certain favored persons who have received apostolical succession directly from Judas Iscariot. This episcopal confirmation, when men pretend that it confers grace, is an infamous piece of juggling. The whole thing is an abomination.

Only to think that in this nineteenth century there should be men who preach up salvation by sacraments, and salvation by themselves forsooth! Why, sirs, it is surely too late in the day to come to us with this drivel! Priestcraft, let us hope, is an anachronism, and the sacramental theory out of date. These things might have done for those who could not read and for the days when books were scarce, but ever since the day when the glorious Luther was helped by God to proclaim with thunderclaps the emancipating truth, "By grace are you saved, through faith, and that not of yourselves, it is the gift of God," there has been too much light for these Popish owls. Let them go back to their ivy-mantled towers and complain to the moon of those who spoiled of old their kingdom of darkness. Let shaven crowns go to Bedlam and scarlet hats to the scarlet harlot, but let not Englishmen yield them respect. Modern Tractarianism is a bastard Popery, too mean, too shifty, too double-dealing to delude men of honest minds.

If we win souls, it shall be by other arts than Jesuits and shavelings can teach us. Trust not in any man who pretends to priesthood. Priests are liars by trade and deceivers by profession. We cannot save souls in their theatrical way and do not want to do so, for we know that with such jugglery as that, Satan will hold the best hand and laugh at priests as he turns the cards against them at the last.

How do we win souls, then? Why, the word "win" has a better meaning far. It is used in warfare. Warriors win cities and provinces. Now, to win a soul is a much more difficult thing than to win a city. Observe the earnest soul winner at his work, how cautiously he seeks his great Captain's directions to know when to hang out the white flag to invite the heart to surrender to the sweet love of a dying Savior; when, at the proper time, to hang out the black flag of threatening, showing that if grace be not received, judgment will surely follow; and when to unfurl, with dread reluctance, the red flag of the terrors of God against stubborn, impenitent souls.

The soul winner has to sit down before a soul as a great captain before a walled town, to draw his lines of circumvallation, to cast up his intrenchments and fix his batteries. He must not advance too fast or he may overdo the fighting; he must not move too slowly, for he may seem not to be in earnest and may do mischief. Then he must know which gate to attack, how to plant his guns at Ear-gate, and how to discharge them. How, sometimes, to keep the batteries going day and night with red-hot shot, if perhaps he may make a breach in the wall. At other times to lay by and cease, and then on a sudden to open all the batteries with terrific violence, if peradventure he may take the soul by surprise or cast in a truth when it was not expected, to burst like a shell in the soul, and do damage to the dominions of sin.

The Christian soldier must know how to advance by little and little, to sap that prejudice, to undermine that old enmity, to blow into the air that lust, and at the last to storm the citadel. It is his to throw the scaling ladder up and to have his ears gladdened as he hears a clicking on the wall of the heart, telling that the scaling ladder has grasped and has gained firm hold. And then, with his saber between his teeth, to climb up, spring on the man, slay his unbelief in the name of God, capture the city, and run up the blood-red flag of the cross of Christ and say, "The heart is won, won for Christ at last."

This needs a warrior well trained—a master in his art. After many days' attack, many weeks of waiting, many an hour of storming by prayer and battering by entreaty to carry the Malakoff of depravity. This is the work; this the difficulty. It takes no fool to do this. God's grace must make a man wise thus to capture Mansoul, to lead its captivity captive, and open wide the heart's gates that the Prince Immanuel may come in. This is winning a soul.

The word "win" was commonly used among the ancients to signify winning in the wrestling match. When the Greek sought to win the laurel, or the ivy crown, he was compelled a long time before to put himself through a course of training, and when he came forth at last stripped for the encounter, he had no sooner exercised himself in the first few efforts than you saw how every muscle and every nerve had been developed in him. He had a stern opponent, and he knew it, and therefore left none of his energy unused. While the wrestling was going on you could see the man's eye, how he watched every motion, every feint of his antagonist, and how his hand, his foot, and his whole body were thrown into the encounter. He feared to meet with a fall; he hoped to give one to his foe. Now, a true soul winner has often to come to close quarters with the devil within men. He has to struggle with their prejudice, with their love of sin, with their unbelief, with their pride, and then again, all of a sudden, to grapple with their despair. At one moment he strives with their self-righteousness, at the next moment with their unbelief in God. Ten thousand arts are used to prevent the soul winner from being conqueror in the encounter, but if God has sent him he will never renounce his hold of the soul he seeks till he has given a throw to the power of sin and won another soul for Christ.

Besides that, there is another meaning to the word "win," upon which I cannot expatiate here. We use the word, you know, in a softer sense than these which have been mentioned, when we come to deal with hearts. There are secret and mysterious ways by which those who love win the object of their affection, which are wise in their fitness to the purpose. I cannot tell you how the lover wins his fond one, but experience has probably taught you. The weapon of this warfare is not always the same, yet where that victory is won the wisdom of the means becomes clear to every eye. The weapon of love is sometimes a look or a soft word whispered and eagerly listened to; sometimes it is a tear; but this I know, that we have, most of us in our turn, cast around another heart a chain that other would not care to break and that has linked us twain in a blessed captivity which has cheered our life. Yes, and that is very nearly the way in which we have to save souls.

That illustration is nearer the mark than any of the others. Love is the true way of soul winning, for when I spoke of storming the walls, and when I spoke of wrestling, those were but metaphors, but this is near the fact. We win by love. We win hearts for Jesus by love, by sympathy with their sorrow, by anxiety lest they should perish, by pleading with God for them with all our hearts that they should not be left to die unsaved, by pleading with them for God that, for their own sake, they would seek mercy and find grace. Yes, sirs, there is a spiritual wooing and winning of hearts for the Lord Jesus; and if you would learn the way, you must ask God to give you a tender heart and a sympathizing soul.

I believe that much of the secret of soul winning lies in having bowels of compassion, in having spirits that can be touched with the feeling of human infirmities. Carve a preacher out of granite, and even if you give him an angel's tongue, he will convert nobody. Put him into the most fashionable pulpit, make his elocution faultless and his matter profoundly orthodox, but so long as he bears within his bosom a hard heart, he can never win a soul. Soul saving requires a heart that beats hard against the ribs. It requires a soul full of the milk of human kindness; this is the *sine qua non* of success. This is the chief natural qualification for a soul winner, which, under God and blessed of him, will accomplish wonders.

I have not looked at the Hebrew of the text, but I find—and you will find who have margins to your Bibles—that it is, "He that takes souls is wise." This word refers to fishing or bird catching. Every Sunday when I leave my house, I cannot help seeing men, with their little cages and their stuffed birds, trying all around the common and in the fields to catch poor little warblers. They understand the method of alluring and entrapping their little victims. Soul winners might learn much from them.

We must have our lures for souls adapted to attract, to fascinate, to grasp. We must go forth with our birdlime, our decoys, our nets, and our baits so that we may but catch the souls of men. Their enemy is a fowler possessed of the basest and most astounding cunning; we must outwit him with the guile of honesty, the craft of grace. But the art is to be learned only by divine teaching, and herein we must be wise and willing to learn.

The man who takes fish must also have some art in him. Washington Irving, I think it is, tells us of some three gentlemen who had read in Izaak Walton all about the delights of fishing. So they must needs enter upon the same amusement, and accordingly they became disciples of the gentle art. They went into New York and bought the best rods and lines that could be purchased, and they found out the exact fly for the particular day or month, so that the fish might bite it once and, as it were, fly into the basket with alacrity. They fished, and fished, and fished the livelong day, but the basket was empty. They were getting disgusted with a sport that had no sport in it when a ragged boy came down from the hills, without shoes or stockings, and humiliated them to the last degree. He had a bit of a bough pulled from off a tree, a piece of string, and a bent pin. He put a worm on it, threw it in, and out came a fish directly, as if it were a needle drawn to a magnet. In again went the line, and out came another fish, and so on, till his basket was quite full. They asked him how he did it. Ah! he said, he could not tell them that, but it was easy enough when you had the way of it.

Much the same is it in fishing for men. Some preachers with silk lines and fine rods preach very eloquently and exceedingly gracefully, but they never win souls. I know not how it is, but another man comes with very simple language but with a warm heart, and straightway men are converted to God. Surely there must be a sympathy between the minister and the souls he would win. God gives to those whom he makes soul winners a natural love to their work and a spiritual fitness for it. There is a sympathy between those who are to be blessed and those who are to be the means of blessing, and very much by this sympathy, under God, souls are taken. But it is as clear as noonday that to be a fisher of men, a man must be wise. "He that wins souls is wise."

How Souls Are to Be Won

And now, brothers and sisters, you who are engaged in the Lord's work from week to week, and who seek to win men's souls to Christ, I am, in the second place, to illustrate this by telling you of some of the ways by which souls are to be won.

The preacher himself wins souls, I believe, best when he believes in the reality of his work, when he believes in instantaneous conversions. How can he expect God to do what he does not believe God will do? He succeeds best who expects conversion every time he preaches. According to his faith, so shall it be done unto him. To be content without conversions is the surest way never to have them: to drive with a single aim entirely at the saving of souls is the surest method of usefulness. If we sigh and cry till men are saved, saved they will be.

He will succeed best who keeps closest to soul-saving truth. Now, all truth is not soul saving, though all truth may be edifying. He who keeps to the simple story of the cross, tells men over and over again that whoever believes in Christ is not condemned, that to be saved nothing is wanted but a simple trust in the crucified Redeemer; he whose ministry is much made up of the glorious story of the cross, the sufferings of the dying Lamb, the mercy of God, the willingness of the great Father to receive returning prodigals; he who cries, in fact, from day to day, "Behold the Lamb of God, who takes away the sin of the world," he is likely to be a soul winner, especially if he adds to this much prayer for souls, much anxious desire that men may be brought to Jesus, and then in his private life seeks as much as in his public ministry to tell others of the love of the dear Savior of men.

But I am not talking to ministers but to you who sit in the pew, and therefore to you let me turn myself more directly. Brothers and sisters, you have different gifts. I hope you use them all. Perhaps some of you, though members of the church, think you have none, but every believer has his gift and his portion of work. What can you do to win souls? Let me recommend to those who think they can do nothing the bringing of others to hear the word. That is a duty much neglected. I can hardly ask you to bring anybody here, but many of you attend other places that are not perhaps half filled. Fill them. Do not grumble at the small congregation, but make it larger. Take somebody with you to the very next sermon, and at once the congregation will be increased. Go up with the prayer that your minister's sermon may be blessed, and if you cannot preach yourselves, by bringing others under the sound of the word you may be doing what is next best.

This is a very common place and simple remark, but let me press it upon you, for it is of great practical value. Many churches and chapels that are almost empty might soon have large audiences if those who profit by the word would tell others about the profit they have received and induce them to attend the same ministry. Especially in this London of ours, where so many will not go up to the house of God, persuade your neighbors to come forth to the place of worship. Look after them. Make them feel that it is a wrong thing to stop at home on the Sunday from morning till night. I do not say upbraid them, that does little good; but I do say entice them, persuade them. Let them sometimes have your tickets for the Tabernacle, for instance, or stand in the aisles yourself and let them have your seat. Get them under the word, and who knows what may be the result? Oh, what a blessing it would be to you if you heard that what you could not do, for you could scarcely speak for Christ, was done by your pastor, by the power of the Holy Spirit, through your inducing one to come within gunshot of the gospel!

Next to that, soul winners, the preacher may have missed the mark; you need not miss it. Or the preacher may have struck the mark, and you can help to make the impression deeper by a kind word. I recollect several persons joining the church who traced their conversion to the ministry in the Surrey Music Hall but who said it was not that alone but another agency cooperating therewith. They were fresh from the country, and some good man met two of them at the gate, spoke to them, said he hoped they had enjoyed what they had heard. He heard their answer and asked them if they were coming in the evening, then said he would be glad if they would drop into his house to tea. They did, and he had a word with them about the Master. The next Sunday it was the same, and at last those whom the sermons had not much impressed were brought to hear with other ears till by-and-by, through the good old man's persuasive words and the good Lord's gracious work, they were converted to God.

There is a fine hunting ground here, and indeed in every large congregation for you who really want to do good. How many come into this house every morning and evening with no thought about receiving Christ. Oh! If you would all help me, you who love the Master, if you would all help me by speaking to your neighbors who sit near to you, how much might be accomplished! Never let anybody say, "I came to the Tabernacle three months, and nobody spoke to me." But do, by a sweet familiarity, which ought always to be allowable in the house of God, seek with your whole heart to impress upon your friends the truth that I can only put into the ear but that God may help you to put into the heart.

Further, let me commend to you, dear friends, the art of buttonholing acquaintances and relatives. If you cannot preach to a hundred, preach to one. Get a hold of the man alone, and in love, quietly and prayerfully, talk to him. "One!" say you. Well, is not one enough? I know your ambition, young man. You want to preach here, to these thousands, but be content and begin with the ones. Your Master was not ashamed to sit on the well and preach to one, and when he had finished his sermon he had really done good to all the city of Samaria, for that one woman became a missionary to her friends.

Timidity often prevents our being useful in this direction, but we must not give way to it; it must not be tolerated that Christ should be unknown through our silence and sinners unwarned through our negligence. We must school and train ourselves to deal personally with the unconverted. We must not excuse ourselves but rather force ourselves to the irksome task till it becomes easy. This is one of the most honorable modes of soul winning, and if it requires more than ordinary zeal and courage, so much the more reason for our resolving to master it. Beloved, we must win souls. We cannot live and see men damned; we must have them brought to Jesus. Oh! Then, be up and doing, and let none around you die unwarned, unwept, uncared for. A tract is a useful thing, but a living word is better. Your eye, face, and voice will all help. Do not be so cowardly as to give a piece of paper where your own speech would be so much better. I charge you, attend to this for Jesus's sake.

Some of you could write letters for your Lord and Master. To far-off friends a few loving lines may be most influential for good. Be like the men of Issachar, who handled the pen. Paper and ink are never better used than in soul winning. Much has been done by this method. Could not you do it? Will you not try?

Some of you, at any rate, if you could not speak or write much, could live much. That is a fine way of preaching, that of preaching with your feet. I mean preaching by your life, conduct, and conversation. That loving wife who weeps in secret over an infidel husband but is always so kind to him; that dear child whose heart is broken with a father's blasphemy but is so much more obedient than he used to be before conversion; that servant whom the master swears at but whom he could trust with his purse and the gold uncounted in it; that man in trade who is sneered at as a Presbyterian but who, nevertheless, is straight as a line and would not be compelled to do a dirty action, no, not for all the mint. These are the men and women who preach the best sermons; these are your practical preachers. Give us your holy living, and with your holy living as the leverage, we will move the world.

Under God's blessing we will find tongues, if we can, but we need greatly the lives of our people to illustrate what our tongues have to say. The gospel is something like an illustrated paper. The preacher's words are the letterpress, but the pictures are the living men and women who form our churches. And as when people take up such a newspaper, they very often do not read the letterpress, but they always look at the pictures—so in a church, outsiders may not come to hear the preacher, but they always consider, observe, and criticize the lives of the members. If you would be soul winners, then, dear brothers and sisters, see that you live the gospel. I have no greater joy than this, that my children walk in the truth.

One thing more, the soul winner must be a master of the art of prayer. You cannot bring souls to God if you go not to God yourself. You must get your battleax and your weapons of war from the armory of sacred communion with Christ. If you are much alone with Jesus, you will catch his Spirit. You will be fired with the flame that burned in his breast and consumed his life. You will weep with the tears that fell upon Jerusalem when he saw it perishing, and if you cannot speak so eloquently as he did, yet shall there be about what you say somewhat of the same power that in him thrilled the hearts and awoke the consciences of men.

My dear hearers, specially you members of the church, I am always so anxious lest any of you should begin to lie upon your oars and take things easy in the matters of God's kingdom. There are some of you—I bless you, and I bless God at the remembrance of you—who are in season and out of season in earliest for winning souls, and you are the truly wise. But I fear there are others whose hands are slack, who are satisfied to let me preach but do not preach themselves; who take these seats, occupy these pews, and hope the cause goes well, but that is all they do. Oh, do let me see you all in earnest!

A great host of four thousand members—for that is now as nearly as possible the accurate counting of our numbers—what ought we not to do if we are all alive and all in earnest! But such a host without the spirit of enthusiasm becomes a mere mob, an unwieldy mass, out of which mischief grows, and no good results arise. If you were all firebrands for Christ, you might set the nation on a blaze. If you were all wells of living water, how many thirsty souls might drink and be refreshed!

One thing more you can do. If some of you feel you cannot do much personally, you can always help the college, and there it is that we find tongues for the dumb. Our young men are called out by God to preach; we give them some little education and training, and then away they go to Australia, to Canada, to the islands of the sea, to Scotland, to Wales, and throughout England, preaching the Word. And it is often, it must be often, a consolation to some of you to think that if you have not spoken with your own tongues as you could desire, you have at least spoken by the tongues of others, so that through you the Word of God has been sounded abroad throughout all this region.

Beloved, there is one question I will ask, and I have done, and that is, Are your own souls won? You cannot win others else. Are you yourselves saved? My hearers, every one of you under that gallery there, and you behind here, are you yourselves saved? What if this night you should have to answer that question to another and greater than I am? What if the bony finger of the last great orator should be uplifted instead of mine? What if his unconquerable eloquence should turn those bones to stone, glaze those eyes, and make the blood chill in your veins? Could you hope, in your last extremity, that you were saved? If not saved, how will you ever be? When will you be saved if not now? Will any time be better than now? The way to be saved is simply to trust in what the Son of Man did when he became man and suffered the punishment for all those who trust him. For all his people, Christ was a substitute. His people are those who trust him.

If you trust him, he was punished for your sins, and you cannot be punished for them, for God cannot punish sin twice, first in Christ and then in you. If you trust Jesus, who now lives at the right hand of God, you are this moment pardoned, and you shall forever be saved. O that you would trust him now! Perhaps it may be now or never with you. May it be now, even now, and then, trusting in Jesus, dear friends, you will have no need to hesitate when the question is asked, "Are you saved?" For you can answer, "Ay, that I am, for it is written, 'He that believes in him is not condemned.'" Trust him, then, trust him now, and then God help you to be a soul winner, and you shall be wise, and God shall be glorified.

Messengers Wanted[7]

"Also I heard the voice of the Lord, saying,
'Whom shall I send, and who will go for us?'
Then said I, 'Here am I; send me.'"
(Isaiah 6:8)

God's great remedy for man's ruin of man is the sacrifice of his dear Son. He proclaims to the sons of men that only by the atonement of Jesus can they be reconciled unto himself. In order that this remedy should be of any avail to any man, he must receive it by faith, for without faith men perish even under the gospel dispensation. Now, there cannot be

---

7. Published in *Metropolitan Tabernacle Pulpit*, Vol. 12 in 1866 by Charles Spurgeon. This is sermon 687, delivered on April 22, 1866.

faith without hearing, for, according to God's arrange-ment, "faith comes by hearing, and hearing by the word of God." Then arises the serious enquiry, "How can they hear without a preacher?"

To this practical point the matter is brought—there must be a proclamation of the message of mercy, or men cannot know it, cannot believe it, and con-sequently cannot be benefited by it. The great con-necting link sought for in the text is a messenger to bear the tidings of salvation, and the enquiry of the olden time is the question of today also, "Whom shall I send, and who will go for us?" The word of this sal-vation avails not until it is declared in the ear. It must be published, or men cannot hear it; and not hearing, they cannot believe; and not believing, they cannot be saved.

There is at the present moment great lack of men to tell out the story of the cross of Jesus Christ, and many considerations press that lack upon our hearts Think, dear friends, how many voices all mingle into this one—"Who will go for us?" Listen this morn-ing to the wounds of Jesus, as they plaintively cry, "How shall we be rewarded? How shall the precious drops of blood be made available to redeem the souls of men unless loving lips shall go for us to claim by right those who have been redeemed by blood?" The blood of Jesus cries like Abel's blood from the ground, "Whom shall I send?" and his wounds repeat the question, "Who will go for us?"

Does not the purpose of the eternal Father also join with solemn voice in this demand? The Lord has decreed a multitude unto eternal life. He has purposed, with a purpose that cannot be changed or frustrated, that a multitude whom no man can number shall be the reward of the Savior's travail. But how can these decrees be fulfilled except by the sending forth of the gospel, for it is through the gospel, and through the gospel alone, that salvation can come to the sons of men. Methinks I hear the awful voice of the purpose mingling with the piercing cry of the cross, appealing to us to declare the word of life. I see the handwriting of old eternity bound in one volume with the crimson writing of Calvary, and both together write out most legibly the pressing question, Who shall go for us to bring home the elect and redeemed ones?

The very sins of men, horrible as they are to think upon, may be made an argument for proclaiming the gospel. Oh the cruel and ravenous sins that destroy the sons of men and rend their choicest joys in pieces! When I see monstrous lusts defiling the temple of God and gods many and lords many usurping the throne of the Almighty, I can hear aloud the cry,

"Who will go for us?" Do not perishing souls suggest to us the question of the text? Men are going down to the grave, perishing for lack of knowledge, the tomb engulfs them, eternity swallows them up, and in the dark they die without a glimmer of hope. No candle of the Lord ever shines upon their faces. By these perishing souls we implore you this morning to feel that heralds of the cross are wanted, wanted lest these souls be ruined everlastingly, wanted that they may be lifted up from the dunghill of their corruption and made to sit among princes redeemed by Christ Jesus. The cry swells into a wail of mighty pathetic pleading. All time echoes it, and all eternity prolongs it, while heaven, earth, and hell give weight to the chorus.

Beloved, there are two forms of missionary enterprise, conducted by two classes of agents. I so divide them merely for the occasion; they are really not divided by any rigid boundary. The first is the agency of those specially dedicated to the ministry of the word, who give themselves wholly to it, who are able by the generous effort of the Christian church or by their own means to set their whole time apart for the great work of teaching the truth. As there are but few in this assembly who can do this, I shall not translate my text in its reference to ministers, although it has a loud voice to such, but I shall rather refer to another and equally useful form of agency, namely, the Christian church as a whole, the believers who, while following their secular avocations, are heralds for Christ and missionaries for the cross. Such are wanted here, such are needed in our colonies, such might find ample room in the great world of heathendom, men and women, who, if they did not stand up beneath the tree to address the assembled throng, would preach in the workshop; who, if they did not teach the hundreds, would at the fireside instruct the twos and threes.

We want both sorts of laborers, but I may do more good on this present occasion by stirring up this second sort, for though all of you cannot become preachers, for if all were and talked at random like the Plymouthites, the church would become a mere vacuum, a huge gaping void. You may all be teachers of Christ in another sense. You can all give yourself to the work of God in your own calling and promote your Master's glory perseveringly in your daily vocations. I lift up an earnest cry in God's name for consecrated men and women who, not needing to wait till the church's hands can support them, shall support themselves with their own hands and yet minister for Christ Jesus wherever providence may have cast their lot.

Coming at once to the text, we shall first of all have a little to say concerning the person wanted; secondly, about the persons offering themselves; and thirdly, upon the work which they will be called to do.

The Person Wanted

The person wanted is viewed from two points. He has a character bearing two aspects. The person wanted has a divine side: "Whom shall I send?" Then he has a human aspect: "Who will go for us?" But the two meet together—the human and divine unite—in the last words, "for us." Here is a man, nothing more than a man of human instincts, but clad through divine grace with superhuman, even with divine, authority.

Let us look, then, at this two-sided person. He is divinely chosen: "Whom shall I send? As if in the eternal counsels this had once been a question, "Who shall be the chosen man, who shall be the object of my eternal love, and in consequence thereof shall have this grace given him that he should tell to others the unsearchable riches of Christ?" Beloved, what a mercy is it to us who are believers that to us this is no more a question. For sovereignty has pitched upon us and eternal mercy—not for anything good in us but simply because God would have it so—has selected us that we may bring forth fruit unto his name.

As we hear the question, let us listen to the Savior's exposition of it. "You have not chosen me, but I have chosen you and ordained you that you should go and bring forth fruit, and that your fruit should remain." It is from the fountain of election that all mercies spring. You may always trace the rivulets and brooks of loving-kindness up to the overflowing well-head of everlasting love. You will find every streamlet, yea and every drop of covenant grace, comes springing up from the mighty deeps of the eternal and immutable decree of God the Father concerning his chosen ones in the person of Christ Jesus. The workers for the living God are a people chosen by the Most High. He sends whom he wills, he makes choice of this man and not another and in every case exercises his own sovereign will. He gives no account of his matters but answers once for all to every carping criticism, "May I not do as I will with mine own? Is your eye evil because I am good?"

This question indicates a person cheerfully willing, and this is what I meant by the human side of the messenger. "Who will go for us?" The man sought for is one who will go with ready mind. There were no need to ask who will go if a mere slave or machine without a will could be sent. Beloved, the purpose of God does not violate the free agency or even the free will of man. Man is saved by the will of God, but man is made willing to be so saved. The fault is not in the hyper-Calvinist that he insists upon sovereignty nor in the Arminian that he is so violent for free agency; the fault is in both of them, because they cannot see more truths than one and do not admit that truth is not the exclusive property of either. For God is a sovereign, and at the same time man is a responsible free agent.

Many among us are perpetually seeking to reconcile truths that probably never can be reconciled except in the divine mind. I thank God that I believe many things that I do not even wish to understand. I am weary and sick of arguing, and understanding, and misunderstanding. I find it true rest and joy, like a little child, to believe what God has revealed and to let others do the puzzling and the reasoning. If I could comprehend the whole of revelation, I could scarcely believe it to be divine, but inasmuch as many of its doctrines are too deep for me and the whole scheme is too vast to be reduced to a system, I thank and bless God that he has deigned to display before me a revelation far exceeding my poor limited abilities.

I believe that every man who has Jesus has him as a matter of his own choice; it is true it is caused by grace, but it is there—it is there. Ask any man whether he is a Christian against his will, and he will tell you certainly not, for he loves the Lord and delights in his law after the inward. Your people are not led unwillingly to you in chains, O Jesus, but your people shall be willing in the day of your power. We willingly choose Christ because he has from of old chosen us.

In the matter of holy work, every man who becomes a worker for Jesus is so because he was chosen to work for him, but he would be a very poor worker if he himself had not chosen to work for Jesus. I can say that I believe God ordained me to preach the gospel and that I preach it by his will, but I am sure I preach it with my own, for it is to me the most delightful work in all the world, and if I could exchange with an emperor, I would not consent to be so lowered. To preach the gospel of Jesus Christ is one of the sweetest and noblest employments, and even an angel might desire to be engaged in it. The true worker for God must be impelled by divine election, but yet he must make and will make, by divine grace, his own election of his work. Here are the persons wanted.

Are there not many such persons here this morning who feel "God has chosen me to do something for him; woe is unto me if I preach not the gospel"? But who, on the other hand, can testify, "I choose the work too. For Christ's sake, whether it be teaching in the Sabbath school, tract distributing, talking to ones or twos, or whatever it may be, my God, I choose the vocation. Help me to follow it heartily, for it is a ray of delight to do your will, O God." Here is the divine side then: the man is chosen; but there is also the human side: the man is led to choose the engagement for himself.

The two meet together in this—the man is sent by the Three One, who here asks, "Who will go for us?" Every faithful Christian laborer labors for God. Brothers, when we tell others the story of the cross, we speak for God the Father. It is through our lips that the prodigal son must be reminded that the hired servants have bread enough and to spare. It may be through us that he will be shown his rags and his disgrace; through us he will discover more clearly the disgrace of feeding swine. The Spirit of God is the efficient agent, but it is by us that he may work. It is by us that the divine Father falls upon the neck of his prodigal child. He does it, but it is through the teaching of his Word in some form or other. The promises are spoken by our lips; the sweet invitations are delivered by our tongues. We, as though God did beseech them by us, are to pray them in Christ's stead to be reconciled to God. God the Father says to you, my dear hearers, who know and love him, "Will you go for me and be an ambassador for me?"

Nor must we forget our tender Redeemer. He is not here, for he is risen. He will come again, but meanwhile he asks for someone to speak for him, someone to tell Jerusalem that her iniquity is forgiven, to tell his murderers that he prays for them, "Father, forgive them," to assure the blood bought that they are redeemed, to proclaim liberty to the captive and the opening of the prison doors to them that are bound. Jesus from his throne of glory says, "Who will go for me and be a speaker for me?"

Moreover, that blessed Spirit, under whose dispensatorial power we live at the present hour, he has no voice to speak to the sons of men audibly except by his people. And though he works invisibly and mysteriously in the saints, yet he chooses loving hearts, compassionate lips, and tearful eyes to be the means of benediction. The Spirit descends like the cloven tongue, but he sits upon disciples. There is no resting place for the Spirit of God nowadays within walls and even the heaven of heavens contains him not, but he enthrones himself within his people. He makes us God-bearers, and he speaks through us as through a trumpet to the sons of men. So that the adorable Trinity cry to you, you blood-bought, blood-redeemed sons of God, and say, "Are you seeking to promote our glory? Are you effecting our purposes? Are you winning those purchased by our eternal sacrifice?" Turning to the church here assembled, the Lord pronounces those ancient questions, "Whom shall I send? Who will go for us?"

I was very pleased yesterday in looking over a certificate of membership I received from a church in New York concerning one of its members who was a sailor. I was pleased to observe that at the back of the certificate there were directions given to the member, and the first one was this: "You are to remember that as a member of this church going upon a voyage, you are sent by us as a missionary. You are to understand that you and every other member of the church are bound to spread abroad the Savior's name." Such sentiments are not only right, but we desire to them enforce constantly.

We would say to every church member, Come, come, you are not to employ a minister to do your work for you. You are not merely to give your half guinea or whatever it may be to the Missionary Society and say, "I have done all." No, but you are to answer this question for yourself, Will you go for God? Do you feel that you are sent by him, not to India, not to Jamaica, not to the South Seas it may be, but into those streets of London, into that court where you live? Will you go among those cottages where you dwell or down in that street where you reside? Will you go for God, feeling that God chose you and that you chose his work cheerfully and that now, by the grace of God, while you live and until you die, you will deliver the message of the great salvation that Jesus Christ has provided for the sons of men? Thus have we portrayed the men who are needed.

The Person Offering Himself

The person offering himself is described in the chapter at very great length—he must be an Isaiah. Being an Isaiah, he must in the first place have felt his own unworthiness. My brother, my sister, if you are to be made useful by God in soul winning, you must pass through the experience Isaiah describes in the chapter before us. You must have cried in bitterness of spirit, "Woe is me, for I am a man of unclean lips!" God will never fill you with himself until he has emptied you of your own self. Till you feel that you are weak as water, you shall not see the splendor of the divine power. May I ask then those of you who desire to serve God this experimental question, "Have you been made fully conscious of your own utter unfitness to be employed in any work for God, and your own complete unworthiness of so great an honor as to become a servant of the living God? If you have not been brought to this you, must begin with yourself. You cannot do any good to others: you must be born again, and one of the best evidences of your being born again will be a discovery of your own natural depravity and impurity in the sight of God.

Now, beloved, I want you to notice how it was that Isaiah was made to feel his unworthiness. It was first by a sense of the presence of God: "I saw the LORD sitting upon a throne, high and lifted up." Have you ever had a consciousness of God's presence? The other day I was prostrated in soul, utterly prostrated, with this one word, "I AM!" There is everything in that title: the I AM! God is the truest of all existences. With regard to all other things, they may or may not be, but I AM! It came with such power to me. I thought, Here am I sitting in my study, whether I am, or whether that which surrounds me really is, may be a question, but God is—God is here. And when I speak God's word in his name, though I am nothing, God is everything, and as to whether or not his word shall be fulfilled there cannot be any question, because he still is called not "I was" but "I AM": infinite, omnipotent, divine. Think of the reality of the divine presence and the certainty of that divine presence, everywhere, close here, just now! "I AM!"

O God, if we be not, yet you are! I scarcely think that any man is fit to become a teacher of others till he has had a full sense of the glory of God crushing him right down into the dust, a full sense of that word "I AM." You know a man cannot pray without it, for we must believe that he is and that he is the rewarder of them that diligently seek him. And if a man cannot pray for himself, much less can he rightly teach others. There must be the fullest conviction of the reality of God, an overwhelming sight and sense of his glory, or else you cannot benefit your fellows.

The source of Isaiah's sense of nothingness was this: that Isaiah saw the glory of Christ. My dear friends, have you ever sat down and gazed upon the cross till, having read your own pardon there, you have seen that cross rising higher and higher till it touched the heavens and overshadowed the globe? Then you have seen and felt the glory of him who was lifted up and have bowed before the regal splendor of divine love, incarnate in suffering humanity and resplendent in agony and death. If you have ever beheld the vision of the crucified and felt the glory of his wounds, you will then be fit to preach to others.

I have sometimes thought that certain brothers who preach the gospel with such meager power and such lack of unction have no true knowledge of it. There is no need to talk of it with bated breath. It is sneered at as being such a very simple tale—"Believe and live." But after all, no philosopher ever made such a disclosure. And if a senate of discoverers could sit through the ages, they could not bring to light any fact equal to this—that God was in Christ reconciling the world unto himself. Well may you open your mouth boldly when you have such a subject as this to speak upon, but if you have never perceived its glory, you are utterly incapable of fulfilling God's errand.

Oh to get the cross into one's heart, to bear it upon one's soul, and above all to feel the glory of it in one's whole being is the best education for a Christian missionary, whether at home or abroad. May you have such a sense of the streaming wounds of Jesus that you may hate your sins and loathe yourself that you should have crucified such a blessed friend, and may you with eyes suffused with floods of penitential tears declare that for Jesus and for Jesus only you will live and die. We must feel a sense of unworthiness arising from a perception of the presence of God and the glory of the cross.

It will strike you too, dear friends, that the particular aspect in which this humiliation may come to us will probably be a sense of the divine holiness and the holiness of those who see his face. "Holy, holy, holy, Lord God of hosts!" was the song that overawed the prophet. What messengers are those who serve so holy a God? From earth and all its grossness free, like flames of fire they flash at his command. Who then am I, a poor creature, cribbed, cabined, and confined within this house of clay? Who am I, a sinful worm of the dust, that I should aspire to the service of so thrice holy a God? Beloved, you must learn solemn respect for the service of God—respect for himself mainly but respect for his service too—or you will be unfit to serve him.

I would feel as if holy work were too great an honor for so base a creature and be afraid lest you should touch the ark with unhallowed hand and share the fate of Uzzah. Or lest, like Nadab and Abihu, I should offer strange fire upon the altar and earn my own destruction. Oh let us serve the Lord with fear and rejoice with trembling; fearful lest we should do mischief while seeking to do good and pollute the altar while attempting to offer sacrifice upon it. May we be broken down under the thought of the excellence of our Master, Christ, and may his work be very precious in our eyes! May we turn aside from every thought of boasting and all idea of serving God in our own strength and cry with Isaiah, "Woe is me, for I am a man of unclean lips!"

This is the first qualification necessary for the service of God, and if you have it not, pray the Lord to give it to you. My dear hearers, you cannot go to heaven without it, much more do heaven's work. You must be made to know you are a sinner yourself, or you cannot call other sinners to Jesus. You must experience this disease in your own soul, and you must be made to loathe it as before the Most High, or else you will be a nuisance and an incumbrance in the vineyard of the Master and will be quite unfit for any practical purpose of holiness and grace.

The next preparation for Christian work is that we must possess a sense of mercy. Then flew one of the seraphim and took a live coal from off the altar. We explained in our reading that the altar is for sacrifice and that the lip must be touched with a coal of that sacrifice. Then, being so touched, it derives two effects therefrom. In the first place, the lip is purged of iniquity, and in the next place it feels the influence of fire, enabling it to speak with vehemence.

Beloved hearer, perhaps you say in zeal this morning, "I desire to serve Christ hear and to tell abroad the story of his cross." Have you proved that story to be true? Were you ever washed in the fountain? How can you bid others come if you have never come yourself? Have your sins been put away? "I hope so." Do you know it? I question if you can preach with any power till you have a full assurance of thine own salvation. To teach the gospel with "but" and "if" is a poor teaching. You Sunday-school teachers cannot hope to do much good to others while you doubt your own acceptance in the Beloved. You must know that you are saved.

If I had this morning to recommend a certain physician to you and I said, "I have been sick of the disease that he is able to cure and I recommend him to you," you would say, "Are you cured yourself?" And if I spoke with hesitancy about it, you also would hesitate about believing in the physician. But if I could honestly say, "Cured! Ay, that I am! The bed of languishing is left behind and the cheeks once pale and sunken have now become full of color and of life, and the blood leaps joyously in my veins," you would be more likely to be persuaded by my testimony given positively than in a hesitating manner.

Oh beloved, you must feel the touch of that live coal, you must feel that Christ gave himself for you. You Littlefaiths may get to heaven, but you must keep in the back rank while here, for we cannot put you in the front of the battle. Though God may make you of service, we cannot expect you to be eminently of service. The man who would serve God must know himself to be saved. The effect of that live coal will be to fire the lip with heavenly flame. "Oh," says one man, "a flaming coal will burn the lip so that the man cannot speak at all." That is just how God works with us; it is by consuming the fleshly power that he inspires the heavenly might.

Oh let the lip be burnt, let the fleshly power of eloquence be destroyed, but oh for that live coal to make the tongue eloquent with heaven's flame, the true divine power that urged the apostles forward and made them conquerors of the whole world. It is destructive of the flesh's power as the coal burns the lip, but it kindles in the man another and a higher power of more importance far. May we have such a touching of the lips! I would recommend every worker for Christ here to pause awhile if he is not conscious of having received it. I do not say give up the work, but do pause awhile and get the tongue of fire. If God has sent you, you may have that power if you diligently seek it. Hear this, you who are conscious of your own weakness and seek to be cleansed with the coals of sacrifice and to have your hearts touched therewith.

According to the text, the man who will be acceptable must offer himself cheerfully. "Here am I." Though how few of us have in very deed given ourselves to Christ. It is with most professors, "Here is my half guinea; here is my annual contribution." But how few of us have said, "Here am I." No; we sing of consecration as we sing a great many other things that we have not realized, and when we have sung it we do not wish to be taken at our word. It is not, "Here am I." The man whom God will use must in sincerity be a consecrated man. I have explained that he may keep still to his daily work, but he must be consecrated to God in it. He must sanctify the tools of his labor to God, and there is no reason why they should not be quite as holy as the brazen altar or the golden candlestick. My dear friends, we do not so much want your money as yourself. Your substance will follow when you have yielded up your person. Jesus gave you his riches and possessions even to his garments, but he did not stop there, he also gave himself, and if you will make a return such as he will accept, you must in addition to every other form of sacrifice give spirit, soul, and body—yourself—as a whole burnt offering, saying, "Here am I."

You will observe that the person who thus volunteered for sacred service gave himself unreservedly. He did not say, "Here am I; use me where I am," but "send me." Where to? No condition as to place is so much as hinted at. Anywhere, anywhere, anywhere—send me. Some people are militia Christians—they serve the King with a limitation and must not be sent out of England. But others are soldier Christians who give themselves wholly up to their Lord and Captain; they will go wherever he chooses to send them.

Some professors appear to belong to God by copyhold. They grant a limited kind of divine right to their energies and substance, but there are many clauses that limit the holding. I hope that you are, dear friends, God's portion upon an absolute freehold. You are absolutely the Lord's that he may do precisely as he wills with you. We greatly prefer a limited monarchy when man reigns, but when the Lord rules we desire him to exercise unlimited power over us. Oh come, my Master, and be absolute Lord of my soul! Reign over me and subdue my every passion to do and be and feel all that your will ordains. It was a good resolve of a good man to get as much as he could from God and to give the most he could to

God. Blessed prayer! May we never be content till we get all that is to be gotten by way of joyful experience and holy power, nor until we yield all that is to be yielded by mortal man to the God whose sovereign right to us we claim. We would first spend and then be spent and so be used twice over for the Master. "Here am I; send me."

Notice one more thought, that while the prophet gives himself unreservedly, he gives obediently, for he pauses to ask directions. It is not, "Here am I; away I will go" but "Here am I; send me." I like the spirit of that prayer. Some people get into their head a notion that they must do something uncommon and extraordinary, and though it may be most unreasonable and most irrational, it is for that very reason that the scheme commends itself to their want of judgment. Because it is absurd, they think it to be divine. If earthly wisdom does not justify it, then certainly heavenly wisdom must be called in to endorse it. Now, I conceive that you will find that whenever a thing is wise in God's sight it is really wise and that a thing that is absurd is not more likely to be adopted by God than by man. For though the Lord does use plans that are called foolish, they are only foolish to fools, but not actually foolish. There is a real wisdom in their very foolishness; there is a wisdom of God in the things which are foolish to man. When a project is evidently absurd and ridiculous, it may be my own, but it cannot be the Lord's, and I had better wait until I can yield up my whims and subject myself to divine control, saying, "Here am I, send me." Only be willing to be sent, and when the sending comes, go about it in the strength of the Most High.

I have thus tried to explain who should be the proper person to offer himself; he is, in fact, a sincere Christian, renewed in heart, brought down by God the Holy Spirit into a state of obedience to his Master's will, and made to wholly consecrate himself to his Master's service. How I wish that every member of this church belonged to such a consecrated body of soldiers for the Lord! May those of you who are not so minded be further drilled and trained by God the Holy Spirit till you can say, "Here am I, send me!"

The Work Such People Are Called to Undertake

Isaiah's history is a picture of what many and many a true Christian laborer may expect. Isaiah was sent to preach very unpleasant truth, but like a true hero he was very bold in preaching it. "Isaiah is very bold," says the apostle. Now if you are called of God either to preach or teach, or whatever it is, remember the things you have to preach or teach will not be agreeable to your hearers. Scorn on the man who ever desires to make truth palatable to unhallowed minds. If he modulates his utterances or suppresses the truth that God has given him even in the slightest possible degree to suit the tastes of men, he is a traitor and a coward. Let him be drummed out of God's regiment and driven from the army of God altogether.

God's servants are to receive God's message, and whether men will hear or whether they will forbear, they are to deliver it to them in the spirit of old Micaiah, who vowed, "As the Lord my God lives, whatsoever the Lord says to me, that will I speak." But this is not the hardest task. The severest labor is this: we may have to deliver unpleasant truth to people who are resolved not to receive it, to people who will derive no profit from it but rather will turn it to their own destruction.

You see in the text that ancient Israel was to hear but not to receive; they were to be preached to, and the only result was to be that their heart was to be made fat and their ears dull of hearing. What! Is that ever to be the effect of the gospel? The Bible tells us so. Our preaching is a savor of death unto death as well as of life unto life. "Oh," says one, "I should not like to preach at that rate." But remember, brother, that the preaching of the cross is a sweet savor of Christ either way. The highest object of all to a Christian laborer is not to win souls. That is a great object, but the great object is to glorify God. And many a man has been successful in this who did not succeed in the other. If Israel be not gathered, yet if we bear our testimony for God, our work is done.

No farmer thinks of paying his men in proportion to the harvest. He pays his workers for work done, and so will it be with us, by God's grace. And if I happen to be a very successful laborer here, I boast not nor claim any large reward on that account. I believe that had I preached the gospel with earnestness and waited upon God, if he had denied me conversions, my reward would be as great at the last, in some respects, because the Master would not lay to my door a non-success that could not be attributed to myself. If the God of the harvest pleases to withhold the shower, the dew, the rain, and the sunshine, why then, in such a case as that, he that sows is not to be blamed if he does not reap. But oh, dear friends, God does not put his people to this kind of trial often. He does so sometimes, but if he does, they may always comfort themselves with this: "I have not spent my strength for naught, for God is glorified, whether souls be saved or not."

Now, Christian brothers and sisters, it would be a very pleasant thing for me to ask you whether you would go for God in your daily vocation and tell of Jesus to sinners who are willing to hear of him, you would all be glad to do that. If I were to ask which sister here would take a class of young women, all anxious to find Christ, why you would all hold up your hands. If I could say, "Who will take a class of boys who long to find the Savior?" you might all be glad of such an avocation. But I have to put it in another way lest you should afterwards be dispirited.

Who among you will try and teach truth to a drunken husband? Who among you will carry the gospel to despisers and profligates and into places where the gospel will make you the object of rage and derision? Who among you will take a class of ragged roughs? Who among you will try and teach those who will throw your teaching back upon you with ridicule and scorn? You are not fit to serve God unless you are willing to serve him anywhere and everywhere. You must with the servant be willing to take the bitter with the sweet. You must be willing to serve God in the winter as in the summer. If you are willing to be God's servant at all, you are not to pick and choose your duty and say, "Here am I; send me where there is pleasant duty." Anybody will go then; but if you are willing to serve God you will say today, "Through floods and flames, if Jesus leads I will by the Holy Spirit's aid be true in my following." Now I know none of you can say that unless you have felt your own nothingness and have had your lips touched with a live coal; and if that is the case, then you will say, "Here am I; send me."

Now, though I have said nothing particularly with regard to foreign missions, I have preached this sermon with the view that God will stir you all up to serve his cause and particularly with the hope that the missionary feeling being begotten may show itself in a desire also to carry the gospel into foreign parts. Pastor Harms has lately been taken to his rest, but those of you who know the story of his life must have been struck with it; how an obscure country village on a wild heath in Germany was made to be a fountain of living waters to South Africa. The poor people had little care for the name of Jesus till Harms went there, and, notwithstanding that, I have no sympathy with his Lutheran High-churchism and exclusiveness. I may say he went there to preach Christ with such fire that the whole parish became a missionary society, sending out its own men and women to preach Christ crucified. That ship, the *Candace*, purchased by the villagers of Hermansburgh with their own money, went to and from South Africa, taking the laborers to make settlements and to undertake Christian enterprise in that dark continent. The whole village was saturated with a desire to serve God and preach the gospel to the heathen, and Harms at the head of it acted with a simple faith worthy of apostolic times.

I would that my God would give me what I should consider the greatest honor of my life: the privilege of seeing some of the brothers and sisters of this church devoted to the Lord and going forth into foreign parts. One gave his farm for students to be educated, another gave all he had, until throughout Hermansburgh it became very much like apostolic days when they had all things in common, the grand object being that of sending the gospel to the heathen. The day may come when we who have been able to do something for this heathen country of England may do something for other heathen countries in sending out our sons and daughters.

Meanwhile, till that has been done, let us aid the Baptist Missionary Society, which was distinguished in its first efforts by that faith and zeal that I have preached among you and deserves well to be sustained until such time—and mark you, I am not changing in my own visions of the future—until such time as we can see something better, and that time I hope is not long distant. I hope soon to come among you and say, "Brothers, by God's grace and the Spirit's blessing we will do this work ourselves; it is our work, and we will do it in God's name on our own responsibility." Till then, since we must do something and cannot do much ourselves just yet, let us right nobly help the Society and give them a liberal collection. Last year I asked you to give, and there was one hundred and ninety-two pounds for the Home and Foreign Mission, which quite satisfied my ideas of your liberality, and I hope something like that same will be done today. We need much help. Remember it is for Home Missions as well as Foreign Missions, so that it deserves to have a double portion.

ALSO AVAILABLE

A SERMON COLLECTION

Charles H. Spurgeon

PREACHING

Introduction by JASON K. ALLEN

B&H
PUBLISHING